# The Fascinating Freshwater Fish Book

## How to Catch, Keep, and Observe Your Own Native Fish

JOHN R. QUINN

John Wiley & Sons, Inc.

New York • Chichester • Brisbane • Toronto • Singapore

This text is printed on acid-free paper.

Design and Production by: Laura Cleveland, WordCrafters Editorial Services, Inc.
Illustrated by: John R. Quinn

The publisher and the author have made every reasonable effort to insure that the experiments and activities in the book are safe when conducted as instructed but assume no responsibility for any damage caused or sustained while performing the experiments or activities in this book. Parents, guardians, and/or teachers should supervise young readers who undertake the experiments and activities in this book.

**Library of Congress Cataloging-in-Publication Data**

Quinn, John R.
  The Fascinating Freshwater Fish Book: How to Catch, Keep, and
  Observe Your Own Native Fish/John R. Quinn.
      p.    cm.
    ISBN 0–471–58601–3 (pbk.)
    1. Aquarium fishes—Juvenile literature.   2. Fishes—North
America—Juvenile literature.   3. Aquariums—Juvenile literature.
[1. Aquarium fishes.   2. Aquariums.]   I. Title   II. Title: Native
fishes aquarium.
SF457.25.Q56   1994
639.3′44—dc                                                    93–31691

Printed in the United States of America
10  9  8  7  6  5  4  3  2  1

Illustrations on pages 41, 56, 59, 60, 61, 64, 65, 66, 69, 73, 74, 75, 76, 77, 79, 83, 87, 102, and 104 are from *Our Native Fishes: The Aquarium Hobbyist's Guide to Observing, Collecting, and Keeping Them*, by John R. Quinn (1990: The Countryman Press, Inc., P.O. Box 175, Woodstock, Vermont) and are reprinted with the permission of the publisher.

# Contents

## Chapter 5

# Critters of Lakes and Bogs                          53

## Chapter 6

# Gently Down the Stream                          71

## Chapter 7

# Aquarium Activities                          90

For little Ben Quinn Wheeler Nanke, who, along with his generation, will someday become the steward and protector of the earth's beautiful, yet fragile, aquatic environment.

# Introduction

Almost everyone is familiar with the goldfish and beautiful **tropical fishes.** Most of us have either seen these colorful and interesting creatures in a friend's aquarium or we've kept a few swordtails, platies, or angelfish ourselves in a decorated tank. But do you know what a darter is? Or a mummichog? How about a fat sleeper, or a grubby? Ever hear of a hogchoker, or a stickleback? Or a madtom?

If you've never heard these names before, you're not alone. Not too many people are familiar with the hundreds of kinds of smaller, native fishes that live in the United States and Canada.

These native, **freshwater fishes** may be silvery, greenish, brown, or tan. But others, like many of the darters and shiners, become so brightly colored during the spring and early summer months that they put many tropical fishes to shame! An aquarium filled with these colorful native fishes is every bit as beautiful as a tropical fish aquarium. Plus, there's something special in knowing that all of the colorful aquatic life swimming around came from the lakes, rivers, and seashore waters near home, wherever in North America the young **aquarist,** or fishkeeper, may live.

# The History of Fishkeeping

People have been fascinated for a long time with the idea of keeping **fishes** as pets. Historians think that fishkeeping, simply for the enjoyment of it, began with the Sumerians more than 3,000 years ago. The ancient Romans kept many different kinds of fishes in small garden pools and indoor containers. The Chinese first bred the bright and beautiful colors of our familiar goldfish and carp nearly 2,000 years ago.

After photography, aquarium keeping is the most popular hobby in the United States and Canada. Most of the fishes kept as pets come from pet shops and aquarium stores. About two-thirds of these are tropical fishes. They are either collected from the wild in their warm homelands or raised on fish farms in Florida, Japan, or Singapore. Other popular pet fishes include goldfish and an ornamental type of carp from Japan called *koi.*

Many tropical fishes are bizarre and extremely colorful. That's why they are often called "exotic." As you'll soon see, however, creatures that may live nearby in lakes, rivers, and the ocean can be every bit as unusual and "exotic" as any tropical fish!

# Finding Your Own Fishes

One of the greatest benefits of setting up and stocking a native fishes aquarium is the close contact and involvement you will have with the natural world. It means getting out into the great outdoors, getting wet, and having more fun than you ever expected from setting up a home aquarium.

It's one thing to go to a pet shop and buy all of your aquarium critters. It's quite another to go out and observe and collect all of the live plants, fishes, and other water animals yourself. By doing this you'll learn firsthand about the various **habitats,** or living places, of the fishes you'll be catching. You'll also learn how they are an important part of the

The colorful koi, a domestic type of wild carp, and the strange-looking oranda goldfish are examples of fishes that have been specially bred to be more attractive pets.

healthy aquatic environment. Understanding how the life systems of the water world function through hands-on study and fishkeeping is the first step toward preserving them for the future.

Observing fishes in their natural habitats and collecting them there allows you to study how they behave and survive in the wild. Learning the conditions that different fishes need in order to survive will help you decide later on which fish species to keep in your aquarium. Some can be kept for a long time, and others should only be kept for a short time and then released back into their home in the lake or stream. The study of fish behavior is one of the most fascinating parts of the native fish hobby.

The only passport you'll ever need to the adventure of native fishkeeping is curiosity about what lives below the water's surface and the motivation to go out and look for it. You'll find something interesting and learn something new at every bend of a river or in every quiet cove of a lake. Helping you learn the "whys," "wheres," and "hows" of aquatic exploration, and keeping the creatures you bring home alive and healthy, is the only purpose of this book.

# Chapter 1

# The Basic Equipment

Early in this century, when the aquarium hobby as we know it was still young, most people had only a very general idea of how to keep fishes alive in containers. To be sure, fishes were kept in large public aquariums just as they are today, but people who just wanted to keep a few pet fishes at home were very limited in what they could keep. The tanks and equipment were not very good. Fishkeepers often had to make their own tanks, heating and filtering equipment, and even their own fish foods. Even today, the type of container you keep a fish in is probably the single most important part of the fishkeeping hobby. Choosing the right one is the first decision you'll have to make.

## The Tank

Thirty or 40 years ago people saw nothing wrong with keeping a few fishes in little round bowls on a shelf as decoration. These were usually known as "goldfish globes" because people assumed that only the hardy goldfish was tough enough to survive in them. Even glass bowls that looked like flower vases or large wine glasses were used to hold a few unhappy goldfish or guppies! These containers looked attractive enough, but they were little more than torture chambers for the fishes. Most of them had small openings at the top. Since most fish owners couldn't resist the temptation to fill them with water almost to the very rim of the bowl, very little of the bowl's water surface was exposed to the air. In a very short time, all of the fishes ended up at the water's surface, gasping for air and slowly dying of suffocation. Some inexperienced fishkeepers thought the gasping fishes were expressing affection or were simply hungry, so they dumped in more food, which only made a bad situation much worse.

The amount of **water surface** in a tank, the area where the water comes into contact with the air, is very important to the welfare of the fishes that will be living in it, as we'll discuss later on.

Thankfully, little goldfish bowls are hardly ever used to keep fishes of any kind anymore. Few pet shops will even recommend them to new aquarium hobbyists. Today, nearly everyone keeps fishes in the larger, rectangular glass aquariums.

There's no place like home—unless it's smaller than you are!

You might think that a fish tank is a fish tank, but that's not necessarily true. There are several things to consider before you purchase your first aquarium. All of them can make the difference between an enjoyable native fish hobby and a fishy nightmare. Let's take a look at these factors one by one.

First, there's the matter of construction. An aquarium is, naturally enough, made of glass, but for safety's sake it's not just any glass. Nearly all aquariums are made of tempered plate glass rather than ordinary window

Fish that seem to be gasping for air in a fish bowl are probably not getting enough oxygen.

glass. Plate glass is thicker and better made than window glass. It has no ripples in it that may distort your view of your fishes. It will rarely crack or break unless it is treated roughly or dropped. This can be very important in a fish tank that will contain water, which weighs 8.5 pounds per gallon. Water can exert a lot of force against the walls of an aquarium. If you decide to set up a 20-gallon tank for your fishes, nearly 170 pounds of water will come gushing out into your living room if the tank cracks and leaks!

You can construct an aquarium at home if you're handy with tools, but there's not much point to it. Today's store-bought tanks are well made, almost guaranteed not to leak, and are not very expensive. Most **all-glass tanks** cost roughly a dollar per gallon of capacity—not a huge amount of money! The all-glass aquarium comes in sizes ranging from 5 to 750 gallons. The very largest tanks are specially made and suitable only for advanced aquarists. The best all-around tank for the beginning aquarium hobbyist is the 20-gallon "long" tank. (The term *long* means that the tank is wider from front to back than the so-called *high* tank. It exposes more water **surface area** to the air for the exchange and release of harmful gases.)

Since modern aquariums are not expensive, don't try to save a few dollars by buying a very small tank, such as one holding only 5 gallons. Small tanks are more easily cleaned and take up less room, but they cannot hold many fishes safely. Beginning hobbyists are often tempted to squeeze as many colorful fishes into their new tank as they can. But, if disease breaks out under these crowded conditions, it will spread to all the fishes much more quickly in a small container than in a larger one.

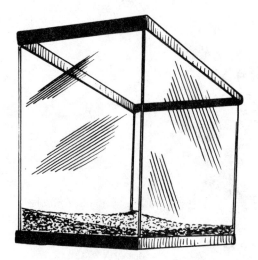

A typical all-glass aquarium, showing the sturdy plastic rim that protects the top and bottom edges.

# Filtration and Aeration

All fishes, like all other forms of life on earth, need oxygen to live. Fishes depend on the oxygen that is found naturally dissolved in the water. In the wild, there is usually more than enough to go around in a healthy habitat. But when fishes are confined in a small space, like an aquarium, the story is different. This is why most modern aquariums are **aerated** (have oxygen pumped into the water) and **filtrated** (have wastes taken out of the water).

All aquariums, no matter how large or small, can only contain a certain number of fishes. The number is determined by the size of the tank and of the fishes, the area of water surface, the temperature of the water, and whether or not the water is filtrated and aerated. Let's go over these important factors one by one.

A large tank of 20 gallons or more can comfortably hold more fishes than a small one. But it cannot be overcrowded any more than the smaller container can. An old rule that still makes sense states that the aquarist should not exceed 1 inch of fish per 1 gallon of water. This means that a 10-gallon tank containing living plants that supply oxygen to the water can safely accommodate ten 1-inch fishes or one 10-inch fish. There are other, more complicated ways of figuring how many fishes an aquarium can house, but this method is still one of the easiest to use. It won't lead the fishkeeper astray!

Even a big tank cannot house a great number of fishes if its surface area is not large enough. Oxygen from the air reaches the fishes through the surface of the water, and harmful waste gases escape the same way.

Water temperature also determines how many fishes a tank can house. Cooler water holds more dissolved oxygen than warm water does. Thus, native freshwater fishes need more oxygen than most tropical, or warmwater fishes do. As water warms up in an aquarium in the summertime, the amount of dissolved oxygen declines. Therefore, nearly all **coldwater fishes** need some kind of forced aeration to introduce oxygen into their water.

Many different kinds of pumps and filters are available today. Some of them are inexpensive and others cost a considerable amount of money. The choice of a tank filtration system depends on several factors, such as the size of the aquarium, the kinds of fishes that will be kept in it, and what your budget will allow you to buy. However, in most cases, there's no real need to purchase an expensive, sophisticated system that may be hard to maintain.

Let's go over some of the filtration systems available today, beginning with the simplest and least expensive.

## Vibrator Pump and Box Filter

The box, or corner, filter and its air pump have been around for at least 40 years. This simple, easy-to-maintain aeration and filtration system provides two valuable services in the aquarium:

1. The stream of bubbles produced by the filter box moves the water in the tank. That means that all levels of water are brought into contact with the surface, where life-giving oxygen can enter them.

2. The "filter floss," or polyester fibers, and activated carbon in the filter remove suspended dirt and debris from the water and keep it clear and clean.

The vibrator pump and box filter combination is the easiest filter system to install. The pump should be located beside or behind the tank on a flat surface. When arranging the tank's decor, you can place a large rock near a corner as a hiding place for the filter box. Some sort of soft cushion, such as a small square piece of foam, should be placed under the pump. These vibrators can sometimes be a bit noisy! The pump is connected to the filter box by a length of ³⁄₁₆-inch plastic **air-line tubing.** The tubing should be long enough to reach the box without being pulled tight, but not so long that loops and kinks form in it. In general, the lower the pump is placed in relation to the tank and the longer the air line is, the harder it is for the pump to push air through the line. Try to place the pump on the same level as the tank and as close to it as possible. That way the unit doesn't have to work too hard and will last longer.

A typical air pump and corner filter combination. This is one of the least expensive filtration setups, yet it works very well.

Box filters tend to "drift" or float. You might want to weigh the unit down by putting a few large pebbles in the bottom of the box before adding the **filter medium.**

The vibrator pump and box filter is one of the least expensive aquarium filtration setups. If it is installed properly and the filtering element is changed at least twice a month, it is nearly as effective as more powerful and expensive systems. It is very suitable for smaller tanks. Vibrator pumps will last for several years with normal use. When they do break down, spare parts are usually available at all pet stores, so aquarists handy with simple tools can do the repairs themselves.

## Foam or Sponge Filters

Sponge filters are a fairly new invention and are easier to use than the box filter. These filters are little more than a piece of plastic foam at the end of an air line. When air is pushed through the line into the filter and up again through an exit tube, it draws the tank's water through the filtering element. Any dirt or debris is caught by the sponge and retained there. This filter requires very little maintenance. It should be removed from the aquarium every 2 weeks, rinsed in a sink, and squeezed clean. Sponge filters are among the least expensive filtering devices. However, they are not efficient enough to be used in very large aquariums.

## Outside Power Filter

The outside **power filter** is another favorite of aquarium hobbyists. It has been in use for about 25 years. A typical power filter costs about $35. If the unit is kept clean and is oiled periodically, it will last for years.

The basic idea behind the outside power filter is that it can filter larger amounts of water than the smaller box filter can. Therefore, the

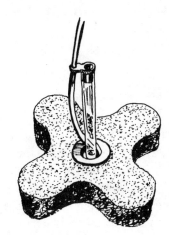

A simple sponge filter. This type of filter uses the force of air pressure to pull water through the sponge element, trapping dirt and debris in the porous material.

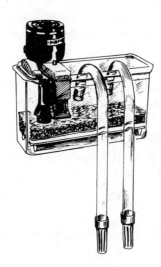

A typical outside power filter, shown empty of water but with the filtering element in place. The more powerful filters, such as this one, have two lift tubes, which are always equipped with slotted baffles. They prevent any fishes or floating objects from being sucked into the unit.

power filter can be used to clean and aerate larger tanks—up to about 200-gallon capacity. This filter has a small electric motor that mounts on the bottom of the filter box. A small, rotating magnet is mounted on the top of the motor. The magnet lines up with another magnet inside the box that has a small propeller, or **impeller,** attached to it. The impeller pulls the water through the inlet tubes and pushes it through the filter unit, then pours the cleaned water back into the aquarium. Some power filters have a small "spillway" that returns the cleaned water to the tank in the form of a little waterfall. This type of filter can clean an aquarium quickly. It also introduces more oxygen into the water than most other filter

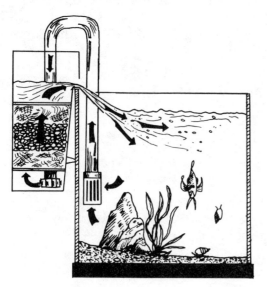

How an outside power filter works. The tank's water is drawn through the lift tube, into the bottom of the filter box by the impeller blades. Then it goes up through the filtering element and back into the aquarium over a spillway that aerates it.

systems, so it is probably the best type to use in the coldwater native fish tank.

The power filter requires a little more attention than the simple box filter does. For one thing, it must be "primed" before it can work. This means that the outside box and all of the tubes must be filled with water before the filter can operate. This is easily done by submerging and filling the inlet tube, covering the end with your finger or a special cap that comes with the filter, and then carefully lifting the tube and hooking its end over the side of the filter box. When you remove your finger, or the cap, the water begins to siphon into the box and fills it. When the motor is started, the water moves in and out of the filter unit and completes the cycle. Most pet-shop employees will be happy to show you the different types of power filters and explain how to use them. It is important that you understand how the filter works and how to maintain it *before* you purchase it!

## Canister Filter

The canister filter is another type of filtration system that has become increasingly popular over the past few years. Canisters look like small cans or drums. They can be large or small in capacity. They are designed to be placed either inside or outside the tank. In this type of pump, the entire filtering and aerating process is carried out inside a single unit. A great amount of water can be moved very rapidly through the system, sometimes with considerable force. Canister filters are best for large tanks or

A typical outside canister pump and filter, showing the movement of the water through the filtering element inside the unit. Big canisters like this one are used on tanks of over 35-gallon capacity.

for aquariums containing coldwater fishes that need more oxygen in their environment.

## Undergravel Filter

The most expensive and involved method of filtration available today is the undergravel filter, or UG in aquarium hobby terms. This system is most often used on larger marine tanks where efficient filtration can be very important. The UG operates on the "forced-air" principle. That is, air is pushed through the system by a powerful air pump and moves the tank's water along with it. The water is forced through a flat, plastic plate buried under the tank's gravel. The filter system uses the aquarium gravel as the filtering element. This system uses **aerobic** (oxygen-requiring) bacteria to purify aquarium water in a process known as **biological filtration.**

No matter what type of aeration and filtration system you decide to use in your aquarium, keep in mind that there is an *artificial* and not a natural process at work. Pumps and filters of all kinds are only mechanical aids to a healthy tank. You shouldn't feel that you can jam a lot more fishes into the aquarium just because you have a powerful filter cleaning the tank. All filtration units are electrical appliances. If there is a power failure in your home or something goes wrong with the unit itself, most or all of the fishes could die before you're even aware of the problem!

# Accessories

The aquarium and the filtering unit are the bare necessities of the modern aquarium hobby. You may want to purchase many other pieces of equipment and appliances, called *accessories,* for your tank.

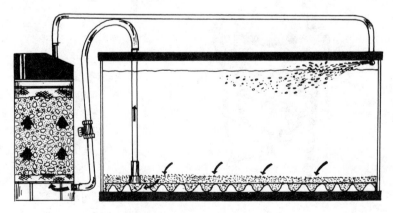

An undergravel (UG) filter.

An inexpensive tank cover and light.

## Lights and Covers

You could simply put a piece of window glass on top of your tank and light it with a living room lamp. But that's certainly not the best way to do it. It is not even a good way! Modern aquarium covers and light units are inexpensive enough so you don't have to use hastily assembled contraptions to protect the tank from dust and to provide all-important light to its plants and inhabitants. When the aquarium lights are built into the tank cover, the entire unit is called a *light hood,* or **reflector.**

The aquarium cover or light hood keeps dust out of the tank and helps keep the water temperature from changing too rapidly. A good cover will also prevent fishes from jumping out of the tank and ending up on the carpet!

## Heaters

You may not need an aquarium heater for your tank because most North American fishes are coldwater fishes that will do quite well at room temperature. But a reliable heater is a good idea, even in a coldwater aquarium. Modern tank heaters are not very expensive. When set at lower temperatures, they will help prevent sudden temperature drops that could harm even hardier coldwater fishes. Most native fishes, except some that live in swift, cold streams, will thrive at temperatures between 65 and 75 degrees. This is the range found in most homes.

You should place a tank heater in the aquarium for about 15 minutes before plugging it in. Also allow it to remain in the tank for the same amount of time after it's been unplugged. Always allow a heater enough time to cool off before removing it from the tank.

## Thermometers

A check of a tank thermometer will tell you whether the water temperature is within the 65 to 75 degrees generally recommended for most wild fishes. A finger-dip in the tank may tell you that the water feels cooler or warmer. But many species cannot tolerate very low or very high tempera-

Aquarium heaters are available in either clip-on (shown) or submersible models. Both are reliable, but the submersible can be concealed behind rocks in the aquarium.

tures, so such a vague temperature measurement may lead to trouble. A good thermometer will help you maintain the best temperature for your fishes. One type of thermometer can be taped to the inside or the outside of the aquarium glass. Or you can use a floating thermometer, which bobs on the surface of the water and is considered to be slightly more accurate.

## Aquarium Nets

Aquarium nets are very inexpensive. Although they aren't really tough enough to be used for fish collecting, they will last for years if they are used only to move fishes around indoors. Most aquarium nets are made of heavy, braided, plastic-coated wire and have a fine mesh netting. The netting is tough enough to withstand most aquarium use. But it will tear if the net becomes snagged and is pulled roughly. The size of the net you buy is, of course, determined by the overall size of your tank and size of the fishes kept in it. In other words, bigger fishes need bigger nets!

## Algae Scrapers

Algae scrapers are among the most practical tank accessories. Older model scrapers use a safety razor blade to remove the algae. Many modern types have a squarish sponge pad that is rubbed over the surface of the glass. The sponge scrapers work well on lighter growths of green algae. The razor-blade models work best when the algae is well established in the tank and is tough to get rid of. Remember to always use caution when handling any tool that has a sharp blade.

The handles of nearly all algae scrapers are long and slender and

The sponge algae remover (left) does a good job where the algae growth is light. The safety razor model (right) works best on tough, heavy accumulations.

usually have pronged ends. The prongs can be used to move smaller rocks and decorations around in the filled tank. They also can be used to push plants that have floated up from the bottom back into the sand.

## Siphon Tube

The **siphon tube** is used to remove waste material that has not been filtered out. It can be made from almost any kind of plastic or rubber tube or hosing that has an inside diameter of about ½ inch. Even a short length of ordinary garden hose will do well as a siphon. But the best ones are made of clear plastic tubing and have a wide-mouthed funnel at the end. If you place an ordinary hose siphon close to the tank's bottom it will suck up sand as well as dirt and fish wastes. A funnel slows the flow of water at the end of the tube so that only the lighter waste material is drawn up and out of the aquarium.

You should use the siphon about once a week to make sure that waste material and excess foods don't build up in the tank.

A funnel siphon used to clean debris from the tank's bottom. The funnel shape of the tube slows the flow of water enough to prevent sand from being sucked into the hose. Only lighter objects such as uneaten foods and fish wastes will be removed from the tank.

# Chapter 2

# Setting Up
# the Aquarium

The logical first step in beginning a native fish aquarium—the step to take before ever wetting a line or dipping a net—is to prepare a home for the fishes and other water creatures you'll be collecting. It's nearly impossible to truly bring "a little piece of nature" into your home by duplicating *exactly* the habitat your fishes came from. But it *is* possible to set up an aquarium that looks enough like the real thing so that your wild creatures will live in it in a happy and healthy state.

## Getting the Tank Ready

### Tank Placement

While an aquarium can be placed almost anywhere in your home where it is convenient and practical, there are a few spots that are off limits. Avoid putting your tank near a doorway, even between rooms. This will expose it to drafts of cooler air that may chill the tank and make the heater work overtime. Never place an aquarium near an air conditioner or cooling fan for the same reason. Also avoid heat sources, such as radiators, wood-burning stoves, or baseboard heaters. These will cause the aquarium to become too warm for the fishes.

Although it may be tempting to put an aquarium near a window, this isn't a good idea either. Too much direct sunlight will overheat the water and cause a heavy growth of unsightly algae. Algae thrives in both light and warmth. Unless you'd prefer your tank's sides coated with thick green moss, stay away from windows, especially those that face south and get direct sunlight!

This rule applies less to windows that face away from direct sunlight, such as north-facing windows. But even here, your fishes will be back-lit by the bright outdoor light and look more like dark silhouettes moving about. They will be much more visible if they are kept under a standard aquarium light that shines on the aquarium from directly above it.

Another very important point to remember is the support, or stand, you'll place the tank on. Remember that water weighs 8.5 pounds per gallon. Even a little 5-gallon tank will be fairly heavy when it's filled and equipped with all of the decorations and hardware. A 20-gallon tank, the size most often recommended as a good beginner's aquarium, will weigh about 170 pounds when it is filled. Therefore, lightweight, cheaper tables or flimsy furniture are definitely not sturdy enough to support your tank safely!

To be safe, you should purchase a standard iron or steel stand designed to support an aquarium. Or, if you prefer, use a *heavyweight* wood cabinet that has doors and shelves. A cabinet will allow you to store all of your fish foods, supplies, and extra equipment out of sight.

Your tank should not rest directly on the stand or cabinet. It should have some type of cushioning material between it and the stand. Cut a piece of $\frac{1}{2}$-inch cork or fiberboard panel (available at most building supply

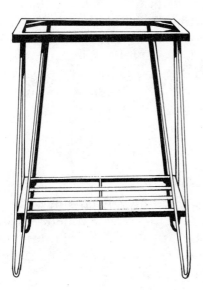

This type of iron or steel aquarium stand can be purchased in any pet shop.

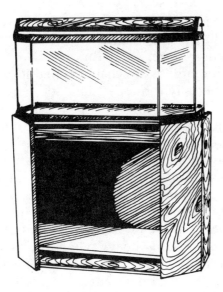

Although you can build your own wood aquarium stand, the cost of a good-quality aquarium stand and cabinet is not very high. It is probably the best choice. Many tank cabinets have shelves inside that can be used as the base for the pump and for storing equipment and supplies.

stores) to the size of the aquarium's bottom and set the tank on this base. The softer panel will absorb any irregularities in the cabinet's top or the tank's bottom and give you a good, solid base. A tank set on an uneven hard surface may twist just enough under the weight of the water to spring a leak later on. Make sure you leave enough room behind the tank for the pumps and filters. And be sure there is an electrical outlet close by for your hookups. It's never a good idea to route electrical wires for the tank's appliances under carpets or across a room!

The aquarium and its stand should be placed on a floor that is perfectly level and capable of supporting their weight. Always place a large tank near a wall, where the floor is strongest. Make sure that the stand doesn't lean forward or backward, even a little. A leaning tank stand means that the floor is uneven. A filled, heavy aquarium on the stand will only make the lean worse. An aquarium that is off balance is a dangerous one that could fall if bumped into or leaned against.

## Cleaning the Tank

Before the tank is placed on its support base and stand, it should be thoroughly washed and rinsed, even if it is brand-new. Even a new aquarium may be contaminated with solvents, glues, or other synthetic substances used in its manufacture. It's always safer to take a few minutes and give it a good cleaning. To do this, use a mild salt or chlorine bleach solution only—no soap! Nearly all kinds of household detergents are toxic to fishes. Even small amounts left on the glass after rinsing may cause real problems for the fishes later on.

Wash the tank down thoroughly and rinse and double rinse! Scrub the aquarium down with a sponge and then rinse well with a garden hose. Make sure all stains and residues are removed from both the inside and outside of the tank.

The empty tank can now be placed on the support pad and stand. Make sure that it "seats" perfectly and doesn't rock up and down or extend off the base on any side. A tank that's improperly seated on its base may crack or split a seam under the weight of the water when it's filled.

## Arranging the Gravel

The best type of aquarium gravel, or **substrate** material, for a native fishes aquarium is usually the least expensive kind. It is plain, ordinary, light brown quartz gravel with a grain size of about $\frac{1}{8}$ inch (a little bigger than this letter "o"). It is usually called "medium-grain natural gravel" in pet stores. The name *natural gravel* means that the gravel has not been dyed to make it brighter and more colorful. Although you can collect your tank sand in a lake or stream, there is always the possibility of contamination by road salts and other substances. Ocean beach sand should not be used in a freshwater aquarium because it contains salts and bits of sea shells. These will dissolve and make the water too **hard,** or filled with minerals.

You'll need about one pound of medium gravel for each gallon of water your tank will hold. In other words, a 10-gallon tank will require about 10 pounds of gravel.

Make sure the gravel is clean and free of impurities. New gravel should always be washed and rinsed well, even if you bought it in a pet store and it looks nice and clean already. Place the gravel in a large bucket and run cold water from a garden hose through it, mixing and stirring it thoroughly with your hand. It's better to do the rinsing outdoors. Dust and dirt or other debris washed from gravel may clog sink or tub drains in the house. You'll be surprised how much dirt and debris will be washed from gravel that looked perfectly clean when you bought or collected it! When the water that runs from the bucket is nice and clear, the gravel is clean enough to be placed in the tank.

If you've collected smooth rocks and waterlogged driftwood for tank decorations, scrub them well with a stiff kitchen brush and rinse them with cold water to remove any dirt or aquatic growths. While it might seem all right to place natural stream or lake objects in the tank without cleaning them, that's often how parasites and diseases are introduced into aquariums. Play it safe and scrub 'em down.

# Decorating the Tank

To make your new tank attractive, you need to become an "aquascaper." Setting up an aquarium involves much more than simply dumping the gravel in and plopping in a few rocks and plants! The more care you take in arranging the decorations in the tank, the more pleasing it will look and the more comfortable it will be for the creatures that will live in it.

## Gravel

Dumping in the gravel and spreading it around on the bottom of the tank is only the first step in aquarium setup. For the gravel to be part of the healthy aquarium environment, a small but important "adjustment" has to be made to it before anything else is placed in the tank. With your hand or a wide spatula, smooth the gravel so that it slopes upward from the front of the aquarium to the back. The depth of the gravel at the front of the tank should be about 1 inch. At the back it should be between 3 and 5 inches, depending on how large your aquarium is. In a 10-gallon tank, the gravel should be 3 inches deep at the back. In a 55-gallon tank, it should be no less than 5 inches deep.

There are several reasons for sloping the sand like this. In an established aquarium, the older parts of the live plants gradually break off and decay as the plants grow. The fishes themselves also generate waste. This material, called **detritus,** gradually accumulates on the bottom of the aquarium. If the bottom is flat, the detritus stays where it is and can be hard to reach when it's time to give the tank a cleaning. If the bottom is sloped toward the front of the tank, the waste material will be moved

This cross-section of a landscaped aquarium shows the basic principle of "shorter up front and taller in back."

down to the front glass by the gentle water action of the pump and filter. Then it will be much easier to remove with a siphon.

The deeper gravel at the back of the tank also allows you to position the plants to form an attractive background. This will leave the front and center of the aquarium with plenty of open space. This open area provides room to position a few rocks and roots. It also allows the fishes space to swim and be easily observed. The most important "design technique" to remember when arranging the decorations is "smaller up front and taller in back."

## Plants

Planting the tank is not a difficult or complicated task. But there are several points to remember in both choosing the plants and placing them in the substrate.

First, what kinds of plants are the best for the new freshwater aquarium? Although you don't have to use live plants in your aquarium, many fishkeepers prefer live plants to plastic plants. They more closely duplicate the living "aquascape" of the natural world. But most plastic plants sold in pet shops today are very well made, and it can be difficult to tell them from the real thing.

One major reason for using artificial plants is that many fish species, such as carp and other minnows, are vegetarians and will eat live plants. In addition, using plastic plants eliminates the need to tend live plants, worry about whether the water conditions are right, or pull them up and throw them away if they die and decay. Plastic plants will last forever. They look good as long as they are removed from the tank about once a year and scrubbed free of any algae and debris that has accumulated on them.

Live aquarium plants can be obtained from two sources: They can be purchased from a pet shop or collected in the wild. Although a good number of North American plant species can be maintained in an aquarium, most of those that are found in areas that have a cold winter season will not do well under aquarium conditions. Most temperate, or coldwater, plants undergo growth cycles in which they die off in the fall and then sprout again in the spring. This process works well in nature, but in the aquarium it can spell trouble. The dead and decaying plants can pollute the water and present you with a considerable cleanup job!

A few coolwater plants, such as *Elodea canadensis,* or ditch moss, and *Vallisneria gigantea,* or tape grass, survive better in an aquarium than most wild plants. But they, too, eventually become pale and spindly because it's often difficult to match the outdoor conditions the plants require for good growth. In other words, although you can get many wild aquatic plants

There's no end to the creativity you can use when "landscaping" your aquarium! Whether you prefer rocks only (top left); sunken roots, old flowerpots, and plants (left); or plants alone (above), you can make your aquarium a thing of beauty!

The two main types of aquarium plants available at pet shops are "bunched" plants (top) and rooted plants (below). Bunched plants will sprout roots if they are placed in the sand and will grow fast if there is a lot of light. Rooted plants can be placed in the substrate in their pots.

to grow in an aquarium, you're probably better off purchasing commercially grown aquarium plants and saving yourself a lot of trouble.

Some of the more hardy and inexpensive aquarium plants include *Myriophyllum*, *Saggitarius*, *Cabomba*, and *Egeria densa*. These plants can either be floated in the tank and allowed to spread or planted in the sand, where they will send out root systems. *Eleocharis*, *Echinodorus*, and *Cryptocoryne* are examples of rooted plants that are usually sold in small pots.

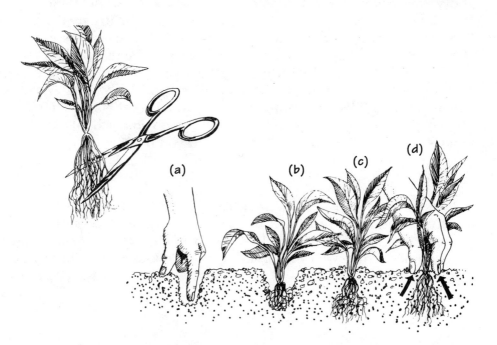

Planting the aquarium. It takes only a few seconds to push a plant into the sand so it can take root there. But how this is done can make a big difference in how well the plant does. Whether you buy your plants at a pet shop or collect them in the wild, the straggly root system should be carefully trimmed back with a pair of scissors before planting. The next step is to prepare a hole for the roots (a). Place the plant fairly deep in the hole (b), and then gently pack the sand in around the roots (c). Don't pack it down too tightly or the plant's roots won't be able to "breathe" and will soon die and decay. The last step is to gently grip the plant and pull it upward so that the base of the stems, or "crown," is exposed above the sand (d). If the crown is buried below the surface of the sand, it will lack the light and clean water circulation necessary for healthy growth and slowly die.

These are planted in the substrate in much the same way that garden plants are rooted in the soil.

Aquarists sometimes differ on just when in the setting-up process the tank should be planted. Should you install the plants *before* you fill the aquarium (the "dry" method) or *after* (the "wet" method)? Both approaches have their good points. Planting dry is generally easier because the plants won't float up when you're trying to anchor them or become tangled up or wrapped around your arm. In this method, the tank is not really bone dry. It has about an inch of water covering the substrate, which makes it easier to insert the plants. The one drawback of the dry method is that it doesn't allow you to see how the tank will look when it's planted and filled. You may have to make some changes in the planting arrangement once the tank is filled with water. When you plant in a filled tank, you can step back and see how the aquarium will look right away. When planting in a filled aquarium, keep the water level about 5 inches from the top of the tank so it won't overflow when you reach into it. Then "top it off" to about 2 inches of the rim when you're done.

## Other Decorations

Rocks and waterlogged tree roots can also be included in the aquarium's decorations. These can either be collected in the outdoors or purchased at a pet shop. If you collect rocks and roots in a lake or stream, be sure to scrub them down well with a stiff brush to remove any debris or possible aquatic parasites that may be clinging to them. As with the plants, any

Many different materials can be used as aquarium decorations. Those shown here include, clockwise from the left, quartz, slate, granite and basalt rocks, curved cork, an old clay flower pot, a gnarled root, and smooth stream pebbles.

rocks or roots should be placed toward the back of the aquarium so they don't obstruct your view of the fishes.

# Fill 'er Up

Now that the plants and other decorations are in place, the aquarium can be filled with water. The water can be tap water that has been allowed to stand in a cool, dark place for at least 48 hours. Or it can be "natural" water collected from the lake or pond in which you plan to catch your fishes. You can't simply dump the water into the tank until it's filled to the brim. If you do that you'll soon discover that all you've accomplished is the need to arrange and plant the tank all over again!

There are two ways to fill an aquarium without creating a mess. An ordinary dinner plate or saucer can be placed on the sand bottom and the water poured *slowly* into it. The water will splash a bit when it hits the exposed plate, but it won't churn up the sand and uproot plants. When the water level rises to about 5 inches, the plate can be removed and the filling can continue without any stirring up of the bottom. An even easier way is to use a smaller container such as a plastic pitcher to pour the water into your cupped hand. (Or, if you have a helper, you can use a 2-gallon pail. Your helper can pour while you catch the water in your hand.) Hold your hand as low as possible in the tank to start the process. This way the water won't be deflected up and over the side. To be safe, pour the water slowly and easily!

Fill the aquarium to about 2 inches from the top, not right to the rim! This lower level will allow room for the water that will be displaced by

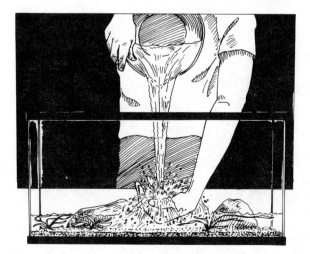

Using your hand to break the force of water poured into the aquarium is the easiest way to prevent uprooting plants when the tank is filled.

the heater and any other rocks or roots you position in the tank after it's filled.

# Rigging Up the Hardware

The main point to remember when it comes time to set up the pump, filter, lights, and heater on the new aquarium is that all of these units are electric and must be handled with caution. Although modern aquarium equipment is designed with safety in mind, whenever water and electricity come together there is a certain amount of danger involved. So always read and follow the manufacturer's instructions.

Once your aquarium has been set up and all of the equipment is in place and running correctly, it should be allowed to stand empty for at least 48 hours before any fishes are introduced into it. This short wait takes a little patience, but it is important that any harmful gases, such as chlorine, have a chance to evaporate from the water. You also can be certain that the aquarium's heater and filter system are operating reliably.

Now that your aquarium's set up and ready, it's time to go and get the fishes!

# Chapter 3

# Let's Go Fish Collecting!

It's a few minutes after dawn and the sun has just barely lifted above the horizon to the east. The air is fresh and brisk and filled with the songs of birds. The spreading pale pinks and blues of the sky promise another warm, pleasant summer day—just the kind of day to head for the nearest water and go fishing! Or, more accurately for our purposes, fish collecting.

Before setting out, remember that the best fish collecting is always done in shallow waters near the shore. Take along a friend for safety and to double the fun. And ask an adult to go along too if you think you may need some help handling the equipment. The more company and assistance you have on a fish-collecting trip, the safer and more exciting it will be!

If you've ever gone fishing, you'll remember that you got up at the crack of dawn in order to have your line in the water before the sun got too hot. An early start is a good idea no matter what kind of outdoor activity you're planning. Before we head for the lake or stream in search of fishes for the aquarium, let's take a look at the equipment, or gear, that we'll need to collect them.

## Choosing and Using Collecting Equipment

The simplest and probably the oldest method of fish collecting is by hand, using no equipment at all. Our earliest ancestors caught fishes that were stranded in shallow parts of dried up streams or lakes. Under most normal circumstances, healthy fishes are far too swift and agile to be caught by hand. But sometimes small fishes and other creatures can be collected this way in very shallow streams. Eels, sculpins, darters, and other small fishes often hide under rocks. If you're very quick, you can sometimes grab or scoop one up in your hand before it has a chance to slither away. But don't count on this method to stock your new aquarium!

27

Most people think of the fishing rod and reel as the standard tool used to catch fishes. Although hook and line fishing is the most common method used, it is not the only way to catch a fish. And it's not the best way if you want to keep the fish healthy. Catching a fish on a hook causes stress and injury to the fish. Although this kind of fishing can be used to collect aquarium fishes if it is done carefully, it is not recommended. If you *do* catch a small fish with your rod and reel that you'd like to keep in your aquarium, always remove the hook gently and handle the fish with wet hands. (We'll explain the "wet-hands-only" rule later on.)

The word *fishing* usually means to catch fishes to eat or for recreation, while *fish collecting* means to capture them for scientific study or to keep them alive in an aquarium. Many different kinds of nets and traps are used for this kind of fish collecting. Let's take a look at some of the methods most often used by people who collect fishes with the intent to keep them.

## Nets

Using a net is one of the best "soft" methods of fish capture. If the net is used skillfully and with care, very little, if any, damage will be done to the fish. The net, unlike the fishhook, is intended to catch fishes without causing physical damage. It is without a doubt the best way to collect aquarium specimens.

*Hand Nets.* The two most commonly used nets, and those that are the easiest to handle, are the smaller **hand nets** and a slightly larger net called the *dip net*. Hand nets (also sometimes called aquarium nets) are most often used to scoop up fishes that are already in fish tanks. Most hand nets are made of heavy, braided wire and have a very fine, delicate cloth mesh, or "bag." The better ones are made of heavy, green, plastic-coated wire. These are best for collecting wild fishes because they blend into the natural habitats so the fishes can't see them.

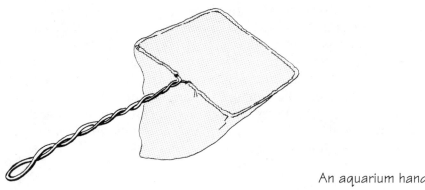

An aquarium hand net.

Hand nets come in several sizes and can be bought at all pet shops and many sporting goods stores at a very low cost. Hand nets are best used when wading on shallow lakeshores or streams or when poking around and exploring tidepools at the seashore. They are very effective when bagging small fishes and other aquatic animals in weedy or stony spots.

The only problem with the hand net is that it is not very sturdy. It may be easily bent, or the mesh torn, if it is poked and prodded roughly or used where there are sharp objects like sunken roots and snags or pointed rocks. It is better to hold the net in position near weeds or large rocks and chase small fishes into it by hand.

*Dip Nets.* The dip net is larger than the hand net. It is the best kind of smaller net for the fish collector. The basic design is always the same: It has a wood or aluminum handle of about 4 feet in length and a ring, or mouth, that may be between 12 and 24 inches wide.

All dip nets have the same general design. The shape of the dip net's mouth may vary greatly depending on the cost of the net and the use it may be put to. The best collecting dip nets, which are usually purchased from biological supply houses, have a D-shaped or a square mouth. The flat side makes it much easier to catch fishes when dragging the net along the bottom of the water. Better quality dip nets have stout handles made of oak and steel frames welded to the handle. They will withstand very hard use before bending! The net's mesh is usually attached to the frame by a tough canvas sleeve or by steel rings. It will last for several years if the net is rinsed in clean water and allowed to dry in the sun after each use.

Less expensive dip nets may be purchased for about $10 at most sporting goods stores. They usually have round frames and light alumi-

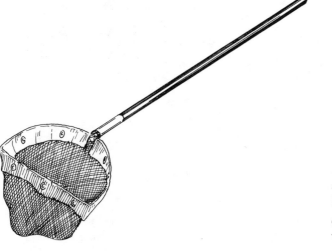

A typical dip net with a D-shaped mouth, which gives better contact with the bottom.

num handles, so care must be used when dragging them through thick weeds or over rocks. These cheaper dip nets are fine for the young fish collector. Just remember that they are not as sturdy as the better ones, and they will not last as long if you are rough with them or use them frequently.

*Lift Nets.* The lift net is another good fish-collecting tool that is easy to use. It works best in shallow waters where there are many fishes moving about.

The lift net is simply a square of netting that is attached to a cross-frame made of thin, flexible steel. A long line is attached to the center of the frame so that the net can be lifted quickly from the water, trapping any fishes that are passing above it. The net is dropped into shallow water and left in place until a number of fishes have gotten used to it and are swimming above it. It can be baited in order to attract fishes to the area. But this is usually not necessary where fishes are abundant, such as around docks or under bridges.

The trick to using a lift net successfully is to get just the right combination of water depth and speed of lifting. If the water is too deep, say over 3 feet, the fishes will have more than enough time to avoid the net as it rises!

The lift net in action. The trick is to use this net in shallow water where it can be lifted quickly when fishes are above it.

The cast net acts like a giant purse when it closes around fishes near the bottom.

*Cast Net.* A cast net will catch a lot of fishes in shallower waters. It is even larger and heavier than the lift net and can be tricky to learn how to use. But once you master the technique, it can be great fun to use on a hot summer day at the shore! Even younger fish collectors can learn to handle a smaller cast net without much trouble.

The idea behind the cast net can be found in its name: It is cast, or thrown, into shallow water and most of the fishes that are underneath it will be caught in its meshes as it sinks. Cast nets vary in diameter from 4 to 20 feet. As you may have guessed, the larger ones are much more difficult to throw than the smaller ones.

It is much easier to *show* someone how to use a cast net than to *tell* him or her, so study the diagrams carefully before you pick up your net and give it a try. Just remember that the basic idea is to throw the net so that it spins and spreads out as wide as possible before it hits the water. A hard throw is not necessarily a good throw. In fact, the easier you toss the net, the wider it spins open and the bigger catching area it has. Don't feel that you have to be an Olympic athlete to make a first-rate cast-net toss! You may want to practice throwing the cast net in your backyard first.

The cast net is very much like a giant purse. The lines attached to the edges of the net pull it shut like a big, closing bag when the main line is hauled in by the net caster. The net's rim is weighted with lead sinkers, so the edges of the net are dragged over the bottom when it is drawn shut, scooping up almost everything in its path.

*Seine Net.* All of these nets will catch fishes if you take the time to learn how to use them correctly before you go fishing. But there is one net that takes little effort to use and almost always catches many fishes if it is used

Using a small seine in a stream.

in the right place. The **seine** has been used as a fish-catching tool for many thousands of years. Although it is one of the simplest nets in design, it is probably the most effective.

The seine is a long rectangular piece of netting that corrals and catches fishes when it is dragged through shallow water. Seines come in many sizes, ranging from the small, 4-foot-wide, one-person seine all the way up to huge nets a mile or more in length. These big seines must be hauled by boats or by gasoline-powered winches on a shore.

Such large nets are certainly not needed to bag fishes for a home aquarium! In between the smallest and the biggest seines are nets that are much more manageable if you are looking for an exciting time near the water and a few fishes for your aquarium. These range from 10-foot min-now seines up through 20- and 50-foot beach seines. Most smaller seines have a ¼-inch mesh size, which allows the collector to catch all but the smallest fishes.

One of the best seines for the aquarium hobbyist is the minnow, or bait, seine. This net runs between 6 and 10 feet in length and is about 4 feet in depth. It is easy for two people to handle.

Minnow seines can be purchased at fishing tackle stores for about $1 per foot, making them one of the least expensive fish nets. These inexpensive seines are usually made of waterproofed cotton mesh, while those that cost a little more are made of nylon. When possible, always choose the better net because nylon will last much longer than cotton when used repeatedly, and then dried out. The upper edge of the seine is called the *float line.* It is equipped with styrofoam floats that keep the top edge of the net on the water's surface. The lower edge is called the *lead line* and has a number of small lead weights attached to it. The result is a long net that hangs upright in the water, forming a sort of moving curtain when it is dragged. Without these floats and weights, a seine would be very difficult to control in the water.

A new seine does not have poles, so you or an adult will have to make them. This isn't very difficult. Nearly any stout wooden or aluminum poles will do the job. The best seine-pole choices are 1-inch wood dowling, which you can buy at any lumber yard or home supply store, or aluminum tubing. Before buying your pole material, make sure that it is not too thick to be held comfortably, or too thin to support the strain of the net when it is being pulled through the water. A dry net may not seem heavy, but a 10-foot seine being hauled through water and picking up all kinds of weeds and debris will break net poles that are not strong enough to take the weight!

The poles can be attached to the net using the "tails" of line extending from each corner of the net. For easier handling, the poles should be cut long enough so that the upper ends extend about a foot above the net. If you've chosen wooden poles, cut notches out of them where the net will be tied to prevent the net's lines from slipping up or down on them during use.

Now that you have an idea of what a seine is, let's go over the net's use under real field conditions.

The seine is a shallow-water net that cannot be used effectively in water deeper than the net is high. The best places to seine are sandy shallows near lake shores and bays. The bottom should slope gently away from the shore and have sections of weed beds where fishes hide. It should not be rocky or have many sunken roots and snags, which can tear a cloth net. The ideal water depth at the deepest, "offshore" part of a seine haul should be about 3 feet. If the water is clear, this depth allows the seine "operators" to see the bottom and avoid snags and other objects. They can also observe plant growth and fishes moving about. Keep an eye out for broken glass or empty cans, which are unfortunately almost everywhere today. *Always wear sneakers or other protective footgear* when seining or wading in unfamiliar waters, especially where the water is murky and you can't see the bottom!

Seining is carried out simply by gripping a pole at one end of the seine, having your partner hold the other pole, and pulling the net along with your partner. The seine should not be pulled taut between the two operators, but should form a big, shallow "U" shape. The fishes collect in the "U" of the net so that they are all in one place when the net arrives at the shore. The haul is always made either parallel to the shore or toward it. The seine "run" should end, if possible, in a natural cove or

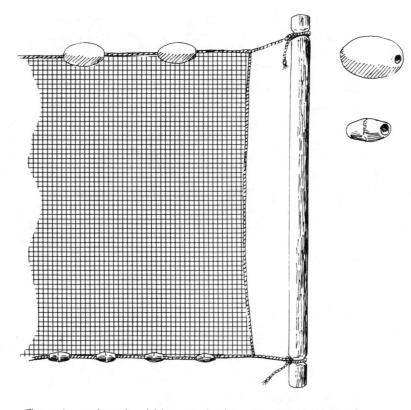

The seine poles should be notched to prevent the lines from slipping. The seine floats (top right) are usually made of plastic foam. A typical seine weight is shown at the bottom right.

indentation in the shoreline. This helps keep all of the fishes that may be in front of the net closer together and allows fewer of them to escape from the sides.

One mistake that most beginning seiners make is thinking that they have to move fast when hauling a seine. In fact, the opposite is true. If you drag the seine at a sloshing run through the water, the lower lead line will lift off the bottom and the upper float line will be pulled under. The fishes will make every effort to escape both over and under the net. Most of them will try to go under it if they can, so the bottom line should be as close to the bottom as possible at all times during the net haul.

Once you've reached the shore, you can see what you've caught and can transfer the fishes to the collecting bucket. In order to go as easy on the captured fishes, this should be done quickly, but not carelessly. Here's the best way to do it: The seine should be drawn up close to the shore,

The moment of truth! Getting your first look at what's in the net is one of the more exciting parts of fish collecting.

but not out on dry land. Leave the net submerged in about an inch of water and sort your catch there. Many fishes will die quickly if they are exposed to air for more than a few minutes. So if you allow them to swim about in the submerged net, very few will suffer and the fish you don't want to keep will be in good shape to be released.

# Fish Traps

Nets aren't the only implements used to catch fishes. Fish traps can be just as effective.

There are two types of fish traps: those that are simply baited and left in the water long enough for fishes to find and enter them, and those, like fish weirs, that are specially constructed and force the fishes to move into a small area where they can be more easily caught with a net. The first type is called the "passive" trap because it is set and left unattended. The second type is called an "active" trap because it involves activity on the part of the collector. Both types will work very well for the aquarium fish collector.

One of the best-known passive fish traps is the minnow, or killie, trap. It is nothing more than a cylinder of wire mesh with an inward-facing cone at each end. The cone has a small hole at the point. This allows small fishes to enter the trap with relative ease, but makes it difficult for them to find their way out again. The two halves of this trap are held together by a metal clip. The clip can be undone and the trap opened to remove any fishes collected inside.

The minnow trap can be baited with bread, crumbled fish, a chicken neck, or dog food, or it can be set unbaited. Your chances of success with the minnow trap have less to do with what kind of bait you use than with where you place the trap. Smaller fishes, just the kind you want for your aquarium, are very much aware of the appetites of big fishes. When they move about they always tend to stay near some kind of shelter, such as rocks, roots, or dense weed growth. The best place to look for small fishes is near or among such protective cover.

Placing a minnow trap in a stream. The trap should always be set in places out of the direct current flow.

Because of this, the minnow trap, or any other passive fish trap, should always be placed next to or among rocks or plant growth or under or near docks. Never leave your minnow trap in the water for more than one day, especially if there are a lot of fishes in the area. Too many fishes jammed into a trap may injure themselves. They may also be eaten by eels and other predators that find their way into the trap at night.

Natural fish traps can be made out of the rocks in a stream. Collect several large rocks and arrange them in a giant "V" shape with the point of the "V" facing downstream. The lines of rocks force fishes to move in a narrowing path. To catch the fishes, stand at the end of the trap's "V" with a dip net or seine. When you've finished collecting fishes with this type of trap, always take it apart and leave the stream the way you found it.

In fact, when exploring all waters make sure to practice good conservation:

✔ Don't litter; pack out what you pack in!

✔ If you turn over rocks or build a rock fish trap, replace the rocks and dismantle the trap completely. Always leave the stream bed just as you found it.

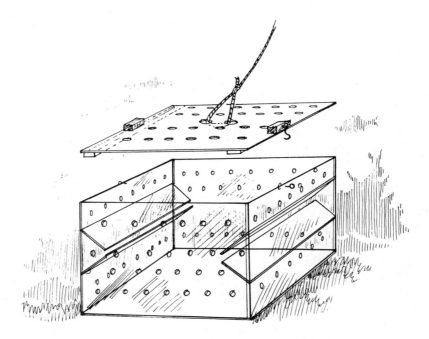

A plexiglass fish trap, with holes drilled in the top and sides to allow water to flow through it. The fishes enter the trap through the inward-facing slots in the sides.

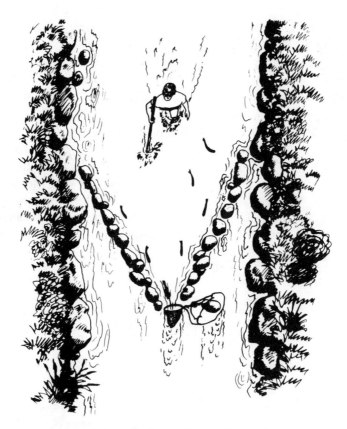

The stream fish trap, from above. The rocks are arranged so the point of the "V" faces downstream. One person chases the fishes into the trap. The second person holds the net and catches the fishes as they swim through the narrow opening in the trap.

# Bringing Your Catch Home

Using one of these collecting methods, you're bound to end up with a lot of fishes. Now what do you do with them? The decisions you make now and how you handle your fishes will make the difference between getting them all home alive and healthy and seeing many of them die before they arrive.

## Keep Them Wet

The most important aspect of handling and transporting your catch is: *Always handle a living fish with wet hands!* Any dry surface that comes into contact with the protective slime on the fish's body almost always removes some of it. Any break in this slippery, protective covering leaves the fish open to infection and disease in the aquarium. The best way to avoid this problem is to fill your collecting bucket *before* you begin fishing and always keep it handy. Dip your hands in the bucket just before you touch the fish to take it off the hook or out of the net. That way you won't add cuts and scrapes to the fish's troubles!

## Containers

What kind of container is best for moving fishes from the great outdoors to the aquarium? This part of collecting and keeping wild fishes is probably the most important, because the animals are under great stress after being caught and confined in an unnatural place. Treating the fishes gently now will make their transition from the natural to the aquarium environment easier.

The best collecting pails are the plastic 5-gallon buckets used to hold plaster and joint compounds. These can be purchased (cleaned out, of course) at most fishing tackle and bait stores for between $3 and $5. When you're collecting fishes, the bucket should have only about 1 gallon of water in it, because these pails can be very heavy and difficult to lug around when they are filled to the top with water.

The transport container can be either a styrofoam "fish box" that you can purchase at little cost from a pet shop or an ordinary picnic cooler. Styrofoam fish boxes, used to ship tropical fishes to aquarium stores, are both strong and light. Coolers come in many different shapes and sizes, but the best all-around one holds about 10 gallons of water. Coolers are made of strong, hard polystyrene plastic and are virtually unbreakable under normal use. In addition, the top can be securely closed to prevent water from slopping all over the car during the trip home!

Keeping the fishes in the dark also serves an important purpose. Newly captured animals of all kinds are very tense and frightened when suddenly confined. They usually react with fear at sudden movements around them. If the container can be closed tightly, sealing out all light, the darkness will have a calming effect on the fishes. They will relax a bit and breathe more slowly, thus using up much less of the precious oxygen in the container's water. Fishes will also tend to remain still when they can't see. So they won't be likely to attack each other or dash madly about the container and injure themselves.

*Give 'em Some Air!* In their natural habitats, fishes are rarely crowded in small spaces. In the normal, healthy aquatic environment there is usually plenty of oxygen stored "in suspension," that is, dissolved invisibly, in the water.

But when we collect lots of fishes and place them in a small container, the picture changes at once! Here, we have a lot of very excited, frightened fishes, all breathing fast and furiously, using up the oxygen in 2 or 3 gallons of water. You may have to take some simple precautions so that all of the fishes make it to the home aquarium alive.

Whether or not newly collected fishes should have artificially aerated water for the trip home depends on three things: how many fishes you'll be transporting, how big the transporting container is, and how long the trip will be. If you collected, say, four to six smaller fishes and will be taking them home in a large covered bucket, the "sloshing action" of the water during travel will be enough to keep a supply of atmospheric air mixed in with the water. This principle works very well in a closed container. In most cases, you'll only need about 2 inches of water in the transport container to hold up to a dozen or more smaller fishes.

If your travel container is small and you've collected more than a dozen fishes, plus you've got more than an hour on the road ahead of you, a portable air pump and **airstone** are advised to keep the fishes safe during transport. Small, battery-powered air pumps, or aerator models that operate off a car's cigarette lighter, can be purchased at any sporting goods store selling fishing tackle and gear. Most small portable bait fish aerators can be purchased for less than $20. They will last for years if they are well maintained and stored in a dry place when not in use.

*Culling the Catch.* Deciding which fishes, and how many of them, to take home for the tank is another important decision that will have to be made at the collecting place. This is called *culling the catch*. It takes real discipline, even for experienced aquarists and collectors, to resist the urge to take all of the fishes home!

Determining which fishes to keep and which to leave behind is based on several factors: the size of your aquarium, the number of fishes collected, and their condition. If you have a 20-gallon tank set up at home and you have collected about 40 fishes of about an inch in length each, you've got more than twice as many as the tank can safely accommodate. Therefore, at least half should be released. If you've collected fewer, but larger fishes, your decision should be based on their size and physical condition. In general, smaller, **juvenile** fishes do better in an aquarium than larger, older fishes. So, whenever possible, choose the "teenagers" over the adults for your aquarium. Any fish that has torn fins, missing scales, or other injuries, or shows signs of disease should *definitely* be released to recover in the wild.

Remember, the fewer the fishes you bring home, the better their chances of surviving and thriving in your aquarium!

# Chapter 4

# Getting Acquainted

Before talking about caring for your fishes, let's answer the question, "What is a fish?" The dictionary tells us that a fish is "a cold-blooded **vertebrate** (animal with a backbone) that has scales, fins, and a stream-lined body." This definition is only partly true. Some fishes do not have scales and many have short, lumpy, or flat bodies that are anything but streamlined! A fish's body shape is determined by how it lives. We'll discuss this later on.

No matter how a fish is shaped, all fishes share one important factor: They are all completely dependent on the aquatic environment, or water, for their survival. Although some fishes, such as the walking catfish and mudskippers, can leave the water for short periods and move about on land, most fishes live entirely in the aquatic world. They will die if they are removed from it. Fishes are well adapted for easy movement up and down and sideways through water, which is much denser than the air that we move through.

Although fishes look nothing like most land animals, especially people, they are "designed" by nature in basically the same way. Like mammals and birds, fishes have two eyes, nostrils, a backbone, and nearly all of the same internal organs, such as a heart, liver, kidneys, and spleen.

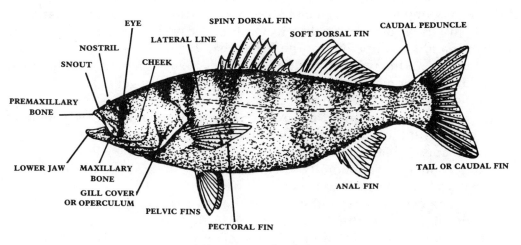

The parts of a fish.

The fish's **pectoral** (side) and **pelvic** (belly) **fins** are special adaptations of the legs (and arms) of a land animal. Unlike land animals, however, fishes do not breathe with lungs but have **gills** instead. A fish's gills take life-giving oxygen from the water the way our lungs take it from the air.

Although fishes may not look as though they are aware of things going on around them because they lack expressive faces, most can see colors the way we do. And they definitely react to other animals near them. Fishes are also very sensitive to sounds in their environment. They may be either attracted to, or frightened by, noises. A sharp tap on an aquarium's glass usually scares fishes, which is the main reason pet shops don't like people banging on their fish tanks!

So, instead of being a dopey, glassy-eyed creature that just swims around and eats fish food, a fish is a complicated living being that has a "lifestyle" just as you do. And it has learned to live in the underwater world the way no other animal can!

Now that you know something about your fishes, let's go over the process of introducing them to your aquarium, or **acclimatization.**

# Don't Rush Me!

Although it would seem a simple matter just to bring your newly caught wild fishes home and dump them into your carefully set up aquarium, doing this would be a great mistake that could cost the fishes their lives. The main reason for this is that most important element in a fish's world—the water.

Differences in the makeup, or chemical composition, of fresh water are very important to a lake or stream fish. Fishes depend upon water for life just as we depend on the purity of the air we breathe. When water is clean and free of pollution, the fishes that live in it are healthy and free of disease. If the water is polluted, it has less oxygen in it. A fish that lives in dirty water may sicken and die, just as people may get sick if they have to breathe badly polluted air.

The water in most natural freshwater environments is generally cleaner. But the water near urban areas may contain many chemicals and pollutants. While most city and suburban drinking water looks clean, it may contain large amounts of chlorine and chloramines. Both of these chemicals are harmful to fishes.

The best way around this problem is to collect the water for your native fish aquarium from the same place you'll be collecting your fishes. The water can be carried home in 5-gallon plastic buckets that have lids to prevent sloshing. It should be well aerated and allowed to clear itself through the tank's filter for a few days. So be sure to have the water all ready before you go out to collect your fishes.

If you must use tap water for your aquarium, it should be stored in a dark, cool place for at least 48 hours before you put it in the aquarium. This way, the chlorine can leave the water through **dissipation** (evaporation into the air in the form of tiny bubbles). Chloromines cannot be removed from tap water by simply letting it stand, however. You'll have to purchase special chlorimine-removal tablets at your local pet shop. They are inexpensive and will do the job in 24 to 48 hours.

Remember—patience! Keep the number 48 in mind. This is a good number of hours to wait for most steps in aquarium setup. If you stick to it, you, and your fishes, should have few problems in the future!

# How Many Fishes?

One of your first questions will be, "How many fishes can live in my tank?" In the early days of the aquarium hobby, when the filtration equipment was not as sophisticated as it is today, people used the formula that 1 inch of fish could be safely kept in 1 gallon of water. Today, if you have powerful filters and forced aeration pumps, that formula can be stretched some but, in the interest of safety, not by *too* much!

As we've already discussed, the 1-inch per gallon formula simply means that, ideally, a fish 1-inch long needs at least 1 gallon of well-oxygenated water surrounding it to maintain its health. Resist the temptation to add "just one more fish" to your tank if your eyes and common sense tell you it's already too crowded.

# Introducing Your Fishes to the Aquarium

## The Drip Method

What's the best way to correctly introduce your wild fishes to the aquarium? There are two methods most often used by aquarists: the drip and the float methods. The drip method takes a little longer and involves some equipment, but it works the best.

You'll need a length of ¼-inch plastic air-line tubing and a clothespin. The tubing is the same kind used for aquarium filters. It can be purchased at the same pet shop where you bought your aquarium and other supplies. It should be about 4 feet long. Since tubing costs only about 12 cents per foot, this will not be an expensive item.

To set up your dripping line, place one end of the tube below the water's surface in the aquarium and clip the tube to the aquarium frame with the clothespin to keep it in place. Place the collecting box that holds your fishes on the floor near the aquarium. The container should have between 2 and 5 inches of water in it. Now, suck on the outside end of the plastic tubing to start the water flowing down through the line. (Be careful not to get the water in your mouth!) Once the water is dribbling down through the tube, hang the tubing over the container and allow the tank's water to drip slowly into it. This gradual mixing of the two waters will help the fishes become accustomed to the water conditions in their new home.

After about 20 minutes of slow dripping, the fishes can be carefully netted out of the collecting box and placed in the tank. Pour enough of the dripped water in the container back into the tank to bring its level back up to within 2 inches of the top of the tank. Don't overfill!

## The Float Method

The floating method of acclimating fishes is a little easier. For the float method, fishes should first be transferred from the collecting box to a small plastic bag. If you don't have any plastic fish bags handy, you can use plastic food storage bags or even smaller plastic food containers.

To float new fishes, suspend or float the bag or container holding them in the tank until the temperature of the water in the bag and the water in the tank are close to the same. Every 5 minutes or so, tip or submerge the container slightly so that a little more of the tank's water enters it. This will help to equalize the waters' chemical conditions. The floating process usually takes about 20 minutes—the same as for the drip method. And once again, patience should be your guide!

## Mixing New and Old Fishes

If there are already fishes in the aquarium when you bring the new ones home, there may be problems with aggressive behavior and wild chasing. The fishes that have lived in the tank for some time will be very curious about the newcomers and defensive about their own territories in the tank. They may harass the newcomers.

The best way to prevent trouble is to use the fishes' appetite as a "bully control." For at least 4 hours before you plan to introduce the new fishes into the tank, don't feed the fishes that are already in the tank. Then offer food just at the moment you release the new fishes. The old fishes will be too busy stuffing themselves to notice that they've suddenly got company! This delay in allowing the fishes to mingle usually makes the acclimatization process much easier.

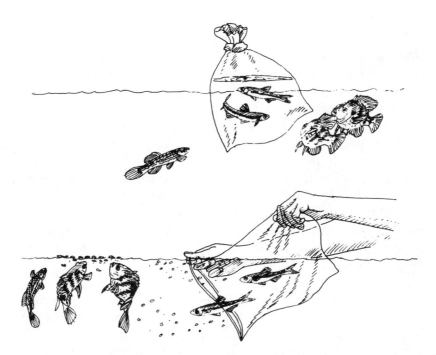

The float method of acclimating fishes.

# Fish Compatibility

Surprisingly, many aquarium hobbyists, even experienced ones, give little thought to the habits and temperaments of the fishes they plan to keep together in the same aquarium. Many people choose fishes on the basis of their color, appearance, and activity. Unless a knowledgeable pet shop clerk warns them that some of their choices may not get along with each other, the result is big trouble in the fish tank!

The reason for this is that fishes, like people, vary greatly in personality, in their living requirements, and in the way they behave. In fishes, this is because some are smaller, **schooling,** or "crowd-loving," animals that eat very small creatures or vegetable matter. Other species are larger, more solitary predators that may catch and eat the smaller, schooling fishes. There are fishes that generally don't bother others of their own size. Other fishes cannot be trusted with almost any other fishes or smaller aquatic creatures kept with them. In the chapters that follow, you'll be introduced to many of the native fishes that you might want to keep in your tank. You'll learn what they are like and what other fishes they do and don't get along with.

## Privacy

Personal privacy is important to all of us at times. We all need some alone time, or a place we can call our own to hide in and relax. In both human relations and in the natural world, this desire, or need, for personal space is called **territoriality.** An animal's—or person's—willingness to defend its personal space against all comers shows just how important it is.

The amount of territory an animal needs varies according to its behavior requirements. For example, cats are predators that generally hunt alone. It's in the cat's best interest to make sure that there aren't too many more of its kind nearby, to keep the competition for the prey to a minimum. Thus the territories of most individual cats are very large. Other animals, such as deer, which eat plants, are much more social and like each other's company. They often assemble in large herds for both companionship and safety.

Fishes can be territorial as well, sometimes very strongly so. In the natural aquatic environment there is usually plenty of room to allow the various species to set up and defend the territories they require. But in the close confines of an aquarium, there may be trouble. If there isn't enough room for one territorial fish to stay far enough away from another one there will be nearly constant chasing and fighting, sometimes with fatal results. Fishes that do not hold territories and move all over the tank may also be attacked and driven off constantly by those fishes that feel

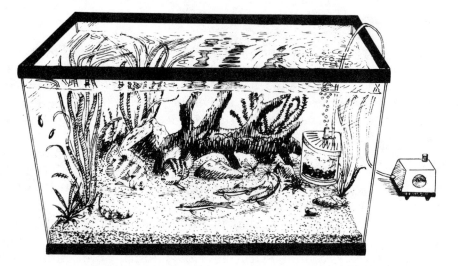

When decorating your aquarium, be sure to provide enough rocks and roots so that fishes can use them to set up small territories. This helps prevent a lot of squabbling and chasing about the tank.

threatened every time they come near. An aquarium that is stocked with fishes that cannot get along with each other is not a pleasant sight. It's more like a combat zone!

Before you stock your native fishes aquarium, it is important to take a good look at what species you hope to keep in it. You need to determine which of those fishes can be kept together in larger numbers and which must be kept alone, or at least in very small numbers. Basses, pickerels, and sunfishes are examples of native fishes that are highly territorial and aggressive. Fishes that are considered "friendly" and can get along with most others include most of the shiners and minnows, killifishes, the smaller species of sunfishes, and most small catfishes.

The main thing to remember is that if you're not sure of the habits and temperaments of the fishes you plan to put in your tank, always stock the tank with fewer, rather than more fishes. At the very least, always introduce fishes a few at a time over several days, or even weeks.

# That First Feeding

Many beginning aquarium hobbyists are tempted to feed their fishes as soon as possible after they're placed into their new home. The feeling, and it's a natural one, is that the poor critters surely must be ravenous after all that time spent in the transport container, with all that jostling about and exercise. A good, hearty meal will help them regain their "old selves" and settle into their new home faster.

But most fishes will be too "stressed out" after being released into an aquarium to even think about eating. For much of the first day of tank life, wild fishes will refuse all foods that are offered and simply hide among the tank's decorations and plants. Shy species like shiners and

other small minnows may hide and refuse food for several days. This is a natural reaction on the part of all wild creatures suddenly exposed to a strange environment.

It's best to hold off feeding your fishes for at least a full day. Then try them on very small amounts to see whether or not they're interested. Ideally, new fishes should be introduced into the tank in the evening and allowed to spend their first hours there in quiet darkness. Resist the natural temptation to turn the lights on to "see how they're doing." Such a disturbance may cause them to dash about and injure themselves. Later the following day, try them on a pinch or two of prepared foods or a small portion of live **brine shrimp.** If even one or two of the bolder fishes begin investigating food items or eat them outright, you can begin feeding on a daily basis.

Fishes, like many other creatures, including humans, learn by watching others. Once a few of the braver fishes are eating, it won't be long before the others lose their shyness and join in the feast!

## A Steady Diet

When your fishes are fully acclimated to the tank and feeding regularly, they should be fed twice a day. Only feed them as much as they can eat in about 5 or 6 minutes. With experience, you'll be able to judge how much to give the number of fishes you have in the tank. In other words, whether you have 6 fishes in a 10-gallon aquarium or 16 in a 30-gallon tank, the amount of live or prepared foods you give them should be just enough to be cleaned up within that 5- or 6-minute period.

At first, dispense the food very sparingly until you determine how much of it will last for how long. It's much better to *underfeed* the fishes at first than to *overfeed!* No aquarium fishes have ever been harmed by occasional underfeeding. But many have been "done in" by dumping in too much food, even once!

The dangers of overfeeding are much greater with prepared fish foods than with live foods. Prepared foods are those packaged commercial fish foods, such as flakes, pellets, and frozen or freeze-dried foods sold in pet shops, or chopped up fresh fish or meat scraps. Any of these food items the fishes do not eat or cannot reach will soon spoil and foul the water. If there are a lot of rotting food scraps in the tank, the water will be poisoned surprisingly quickly and kill the fishes.

It's a little less dangerous to feed too many live food animals to fishes. Most of the tiny creatures can survive on their own in the aquarium for some time. For instance, live brine shrimp can survive for days in a purely freshwater aquarium. The danger with brine shrimp "on the loose" in an aquarium is that many are sucked into the inflow tubes of the aquarium

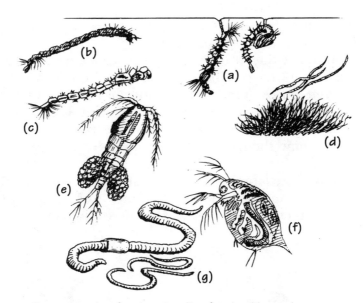

Some popular freshwater live foods. Shown here are
(a) mosquito larvae, which must be collected in
stagnant water; (b) bloodworm and (c) white worm,
which are midge larvae, not worms; (d) tubifex
worms, showing individual worms and colony;
(e) cyclops, a tiny crustacean; (f) daphnia;
(g) nightcrawler and smaller angleworms.

filter. They end up lodged in the filtering material, where they die and
begin to rot.

Tubifex worms are another popular live food, sold in almost every
pet shop. Tubifex worms are rinsed and cleaned of impurities before they
are sold. But they should be rinsed every time you feed a portion of them
to your fishes, just to be safe. They should be fed only in small portions
because escaped tubifex can establish themselves in the gravel of the tank
and be very difficult to get rid of.

Fishes both need and appreciate a varied diet. Just what a fish will
or will not eat depends on the **species.** People may be meat-eaters or
strict vegetarians by choice. But, in general, humans everywhere can
survive on the same wide variety of foods because we are **omnivorous**
(can eat both meats and vegetables) creatures.

Most fishes, however, are more specialized in their feeding habits.
While such fishes as catfishes and eels will eagerly devour most plant and
animal material, others, such as carp, goldfish, and suckermouth catfishes,
are almost entirely vegetarian. But most of the world's fishes, both freshwater and **marine,** are **carnivorous,** or meat eaters. For most of these,

being a carnivore means that they eat other fishes and small aquatic animals found in their environment.

Determining the correct foods for each native fish species in your aquarium doesn't have to be complicated. Although we'll be discussing the food preferences of the various kinds of native aquarium fishes later on, there *is* a simple way to get a general idea of what a fish eats: Look at its mouth. Most fishes have teeth, and the type and number of them usually determine the nature of the natural food, or prey, the fish seeks out and eats.

The obvious examples of fishes that are predators and eat meat are sharks and barracuda. When these creatures are kept in the huge tanks of oceanariums, they are fed almost entirely on whole fish, and lots of it!

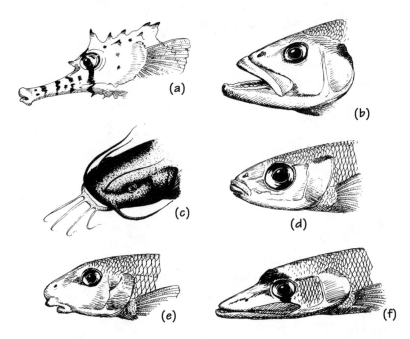

A fish's mouth will tell you something about what and how it eats. (a) The seahorse waits for small prey to swim near and then "vacuums" them in with its small, toothless mouth. (b) The bass chases down prey and grabs it with its powerful jaws and sharp teeth. (c) The catfish prowls the dark bottom and finds food with its sensitive barbels, or whiskers. (d) The shiner eats tiny animals that live in the water and doesn't need powerful jaws and teeth. (e) The sucker is a bottom dweller that eats mostly vegetable foods so its mouth is on the underside of its head. (f) The pickerel waits motionless for prey and then grabs it in a swift rush.

Smaller freshwater and marine fishes might not look as ferocious as these big predators, but most of them are meat-eaters just the same!

Many native fishes are not overly picky and will accept many of the prepared and freeze-dried fish foods sold in pet stores. Prepared foods are available in both meat- and vegetable-based formulas, based on the kind of goldfish or tropical fishes they're designed to feed. So once you've determined what that catfish, shiner, or bass you've collected would prefer to eat, purchase the appropriate prepared food for it.

Most wild fishes prefer some fresh food in their diets. This can consist of chopped fish or very lean beef, or, better yet, any of the several kinds of **live food** you can buy. Fishes may not always get the nutrients they need in prepared foods, or even in bits of chopped fish. But small, *whole* live animals or "feeder fishes" fed to larger fishes will provide them with all of the nutrients they'd get in the wild.

Many of the vegetarian, or **herbivorous** species, such as carp and some of the smaller shiners and catfishes, will graze on any algae that grows in the aquarium. If letting the algae in the tank grow thick enough to feed the vegetarians among your fishes doesn't appeal to you, you can occasionally offer them small leaves of lettuce or spinach as a substitute.

Regardless of the type of foods fed to wild fishes, remember, don't overfeed! If you have **scavengers** such as catfishes, snails, or small eels in your tank, the feedings can be a little more generous. After all, you have the "cleanup crew" standing by to pick up any leftovers! But once again, it is far better, and safer, to underfeed than to overfeed.

# Good Housekeeping

Housekeeping, that is, the periodic "aquatinkering" that you'll be doing to keep the tank clean, healthy, and nice looking, will be easy if all of its mechanical and natural systems are functioning well. General maintenance consists of the daily, weekly, and monthly attention to relatively minor details.

*Daily:* Feed fishes twice a day, in the early morning and in the evening. Check the water temperature. Check for any illness among the fishes and other inhabitants. Check to make sure all of your equipment—the pumps, filters, and lights—is working properly.

*Weekly:* Siphon off any debris and waste that has accumulated on the bottom. Trim back any dead or dying plant leaves. Remove any algae growth from the front glass. (You may wish to leave some on the sides and back of the aquarium as green fish food.) Make sure the underside of the light hood is clean and free of salty brine or excessive moisture.

*Monthly:* Clean or replace the filter medium. Do a water change, replacing between 15 and 25 percent of the water with aged fresh water. Gently stir the substrate, especially if the tank has an under-gravel filter, to help it circulate water better. Check all tubing and hose connections on pumps and filters. Replace any burned out bulbs in the light hood. *Always unplug any electrical aquarium equipment before working on it!*

# Chapter 5

# Critters of Lakes and Bogs

Many wild creatures that can be kept in the home aquarium live in North America's lakes, ponds, and bogs. These environments offer the aquarist a wealth of exploring adventures.

The first rule of all fish collecting is *never go out alone!* Bodies of fresh water, both large and small, are usually thought of as friendly places where one can swim and have fun with perfect safety. But, as with all aquatic environments, the aquatic explorer must use common sense and care when launching a freshwater collecting expedition.

Collecting freshwater lake and pond animals often involves exploring areas that are far from other people. You'll find more aquatic creatures

The lake edge.

in places that are the least disturbed by swimming and boating activity. Be sure that an adult is exploring with you, or at least knows where you and your friends are at all times!

The safety factor is the most important reason for using the "buddy system" when exploring lake and pond shores, but it's not the only one. Observing and collecting lake and pond water life is much more enjoyable when you've got friends along to share in the excitement.

The second rule for the beginning fish collector is *stay near the shore.* Observing and collecting freshwater plants and animals is always much better near the shore, or **littoral zone.** The shallower waters near the shoreline of a lake or large pond are always richer in both plant and animal life. This is because sunlight reaches to the bottom and promotes the abundant growth of vegetation that both prey and predator animals depend on.

Collecting fishes in lakes and ponds can be done using any of the equipment discussed in Chapter 2. The dip net, the seine, or the minnow trap will bring you good results if there are lots of fishes and you use the equipment properly.

Marshes and bogs can be exciting, adventurous places to explore and collect fishes because there is often a great variety of life there. The only potential problem you might encounter in exploring these fascinating habitats is that they can be hard to get to. The land area of many marshes and bogs is not all firm ground. Some bogs are composed of great mats of vegetation that actually float on the surface of the water. These bogs are referred to as *quaking bogs.* If you jump up and down on the thick plant mat, the entire area bounces slowly up and down like a huge water bed! Always check out a marshy area you plan to wade in and never go "bog-trotting" without an experienced adult.

You won't find many fishes in a quaking bog because the exposed water surface is usually small. But other freshwater marshes abound with fish life. Any marsh or bog that is large enough and holds water year-round will likely contain fish life as well as many reptiles, amphibians, and marsh birds. Observing the many different kinds of wildlife found near wetlands makes the fish-collecting experience all the more exciting!

Fish collecting in marshes and bogs is best done at the edges, where the water is shallow and filled with dense plant growth. The best way to sample the area is to simply run your dip net through thick weeds and see what turns up in it. Very often the catch will be composed of many small insects and other tiny aquatic animals. But you might find a small fish or two as well. If it looks as though there are fishes in the area, pull on a pair of old sneakers, or waders if it's cold, and try a small seine near the shore. A seine haul made in a marsh in summer should bag a good number of fishes.

The freshwater marsh.

Water lily beds are also great places to look for aquarium fishes. Water lilies seldom grow in water more than 4 feet deep. Their tangle of stems looks like an underwater rain forest. Schools of small fishes, turtles, and other water life like to hide among the tangle of lily stems.

## SOME LAKE, POND, AND MARSH FISHES

# Bass

The largemouth and smallmouth basses are voracious game fishes that can be kept in an aquarium, but only with care. They are very smart fishes and quickly come to recognize their keeper. They will approach the glass to be fed when they see their owner!

A number of species and **subspecies** of bass exist throughout the United States. They may be called the redeye, spotted, shoal, or Guadaloupe

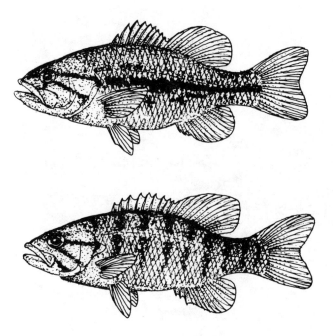

Largemouth bass (top) and smallmouth bass (bottom).

bass, depending on the species and the locality. The largemouth bass grows to the largest size, often reaching 3 feet long in the best habitats. The largest smallmouth reaches a length of about 28 inches. But large or small, neither fish can be trusted with other fishes in an aquarium unless the basses are very small and the other fishes large enough to avoid being attacked and swallowed.

Both of these basses, often called black basses, are usually a dark olive green above and goldish below. The largemouth has a broad, blotchy black stripe running the length of its body. The smallmouth is marked by a series of irregular vertical bands on the sides. One way to tell the difference between these similar-looking fishes is to look at their mouths. In the largemouth, the corner of the mouth extends past the eye. In the smallmouth it ends just below the eye.

Largemouth basses prefer warmer, shallower, weedier waters, while the smallmouth likes cooler, rockier lakes and rivers. The young of both species, the only size that could be even considered for the home tank, are always found near shore where there are weed beds, fallen trees, rocks, and other shelter. Little basses never hang around with bigger basses because the adults would eat them without a second thought.

Basses can only be kept with fishes their own size. They will chase and harass shiners and other peaceful fishes, even if they are too large to eat. The bass tank should have plenty of hideaways so the fishes can set up small territories and stay out of each other's way.

Basses will eat almost any meat or fish foods, alive or dead. They can be given live brine shrimp when they are small and then offered worms, small fishes, chopped meat or fish, and even prepared goldfish pellets when they grow larger.

In view of the bass's great appetite and aggressive disposition, the smart basskeeper will make his or her relationship with a bass a temporary one. The fish should be released back into the wild at the end of summer!

# Bowfin

The bowfin is an ancient animal, having shared the earth with the dinosaurs as far back as the Jurassic era. It is what is known in scientific language as a "primitive" fish because it has many of the characteristics of the earliest fishes that appeared on earth some 450 million years ago. Lampreys, gars, sturgeons, and the marine coelacanth are other examples of primitive fishes that survive today.

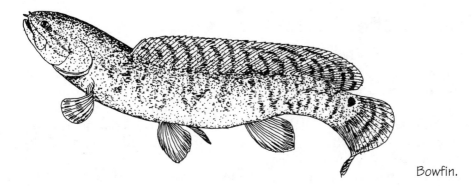

Bowfin.

The adult bowfin is a large creature that looks every bit as voracious as it is. The 43-inch-long body is cylindrical in shape, and the large head has powerful jaws studded with many teeth. The fish's nostrils look like small tubes. This fish is a predator, make no mistake about it!

The bowfin is found throughout much of the midwestern part of the United States and along the Atlantic seaboard as far north as Pennsylvania. It is not often found in mountainous areas. It prefers the swamps and marshes of the Mississippi River Valley and the Atlantic **Coastal Plain.**

The bowfin's color and pattern closely resemble the bottom vegetation of the swamps and sloughs it lives in. It is a mottled olive green above and white or yellowish below. And it has blackish bands and spots on the **dorsal** and **caudal fins.** The young fish are more brightly colored, having a bright orange "halo" around a large black tail spot and turquoise-green lower fins.

Young bowfins are harmless and make good aquarium fishes. They spend most of their time lurking in dense weed beds. Thus, the best way to collect them is to simply drag a small seine through thick vegetation and hope one turns up in the bag. A dip net swept through weeds or underneath a boggy bank overhang will often turn up a little bowfin.

Very small bowfins can share a tank with other fishes as long as they are of roughly the same size. But a large one must be kept by itself. Like pickerels, bowfins wait in thick weeds for prey to approach and then grab it with a swift dash. They are attracted to any kind of quick motion and may grab fishes that are nearly as long as they are. So if you have a 5-inch-long bowfin in your tank, make sure its tankmates are a little bit longer!

The bowfin tank should be thickly planted and dimly lighted. An inexpensive air pump and corner filter are all the filtration you need in a bowfin tank containing a single fish. Feed your bowfin nightcrawlers and pieces of lean meat or fish and it will be content.

# Bullhead Catfishes

Catfishes have always been very popular with aquarium hobbyists. The native catfishes are not quite as "cute" as tropical "cats" like the corydoras catfishes. But they are equally fascinating and will not cause trouble in the aquarium—when they are small, at least. There are 40 species of bullhead catfishes found in North America, including the channel catfish, the blue catfish, and the little madtoms of our rivers and streams. Bullheads are medium-sized to large fishes with large heads, smooth, scaleless skins, and four pairs of **barbels,** or whiskers around the mouth. The barbels serve as sensory organs that help the catfishes locate food in the dim and murky waters they often live in.

Most of the bullheads are brownish, blackish, or yellowish in color. But some, like the channel cat, may be silvery-bluish and spotted with black. The most common bullheads in North America are the black, yellow, and brown bullheads. Almost every angler has caught one of these species at one time or another. Another popular name for these catfishes is "horned pout."

Bullheads can be collected by sweeping a dip net through weeds and debris at the lake's shore or by seining in weedy areas. But the easiest way is to bait a minnow trap with a chicken neck or a fish head and leave it among submerged weeds overnight. If there are any bullheads in the lake or pond, you should have more little "pouts" than you know what to do with in the trap the next morning!

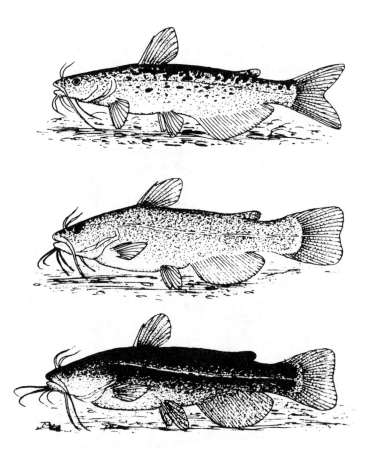

Channel catfish and yellow and black bullheads.

Bullheads and most other catfishes are usually considered harmless scavengers that do not attack and eat other fishes. However, this may not always be true. These catfishes are **nocturnal,** that is, they move about mostly at night. They will capture and eat any fish they can catch. So this means that any bullhead intended for aquarium use must be a small one! If you can get very young ones of an inch or two in length, this is the best size. These fishes grow amazingly fast if offered plenty of food and may soon be a threat to other fishes in the tank. A 2-inch bullhead collected in June may reach 5 or 6 inches by September. So unless you're prepared to feed a large and hungry fish through the long winter months, plan to release the bullhead before the weather gets too cold.

Bullheads are happiest when kept in a dimly lit aquarium. They will stay out of sight if the lights are too bright. They will eat nearly all fish foods, and even such oddball things as pieces of hotdog, salami, and cheese!

A catfish tank should be well planted and provided with plenty of rocky grottoes and hiding places. Larger pieces of flat slate and other rocks and old clay flower pots laid on their sides make good catfish hideouts.

# Mudminnows

The little mudminnow is another native fish that has little to recommend it in terms of color. But its "personality" more than makes up for this failing. Primarily a warm, reddish brown, with darker bands or stripes on the sides, the little "mud trout" is another creature of quiet, weedy waters. It is seldom seen swimming about.

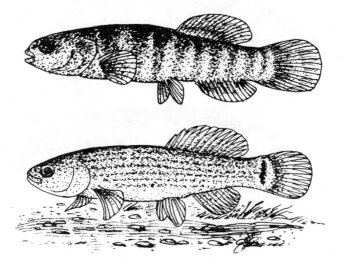

Central mudminnow (top) and Eastern mudminnow (bottom).

There are three species of mudminnows in North America. They are all quite similar in appearance. The eastern mudminnow, which is marked by many narrow bands running from nose to tail, is found along the Coastal Plain from Long Island, New York, to Florida. The central mudminnow has up to 14 dark, vertical bars on the sides. It can be found from the Saint Lawrence River and the Great Lakes south to Ohio and Tennessee. The Olympic mudminnow is a dark brown or greenish fish with about ten whitish or yellow narrow bands on its sides. It lives in a small area of the Olympic Peninsula in Washington State.

All three species of mudminnows are small **fish** that seldom exceed 5 inches in length. They are inhabitants of small streams, swamps, bogs, and other wetlands. They are always found in heavy weed growth or among submerged debris. These fish got their name because they have been known to bury themselves in the wet bottom mud when their pond or swamp dries up. They wait for the return of the water when it rains.

Mudminnows are collected by netting up a mass of water plants and pawing through it. Once acclimated to the aquarium, these fish tame rapidly. They will even accept bits of food from the aquarist's fingers or a pair of tweezers. Some have been trained to jump for tidbits suspended above the water!

The behavior of mudminnows shows that they have reasonably high intelligence—for a fish, at least—and they make very amusing pets. They will stop suddenly and closely examine an object that interests them as if they were thinking it over. Hovering in the water with quivering fins, they turn their heads almost as though they had necks. Although their behavior may appear menacing, mudminnows are completely harmless to other fishes their own size. They will get along peacefully in a **community tank** where different kinds of fishes are kept. They will eat virtually all types of fish foods, from live and frozen foods to tropical fish flake foods.

The mudminnows' tank should be kept well covered as these adventurous little creatures may jump from the water. They seem especially likely to try an escape where the flow from a power filter enters the aquarium—almost like tiny salmon migrating up a waterfall! If you're missing your mudminnow and have looked everywhere in the aquarium, take a look in the filter's box. That's where many jumpers often end up.

# Pickerel

There are four species of pickerels and pikes living in North America. The smallest species, the little grass, or redfin, pickerel, grows to about 15 inches. The largest, the giant muskellunge of northern lakes, may grow to 72 inches long and weigh 60 pounds. Regardless of the species, all pikes and pickerels look basically alike. They are all long, slim fish with pointed **snouts** that look much like a duck's bill. Most are greenish-yellow in color. They have various patterns of dark bars, spots, and chainlike scribblings on their sides. All of these fish are voracious **ambush predators** that lie in wait among dense weeds for passing prey. They do not attempt

Chain pickerel.

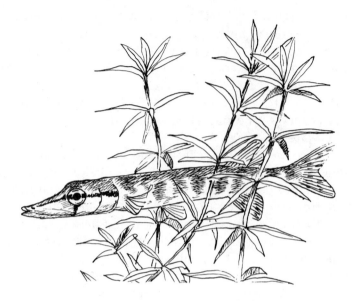

A baby pickerel hides among weeds, waiting for passing prey.

to chase and capture other fishes. Instead, they grab the prey in a swift dash. If the pickerel misses on the first rush, it gives up, returns to its hideaway, and waits for another victim to come along.

These fierce fish are almost always found near lake and bog shores, where they hide among the submerged plants. Only the smallest pikes and pickerels can be kept in the average home tank. Ideally, you should look for a young pickerel no more than 4 inches long. These are best collected with a dip net or a seine. Very often, it is nearly impossible to see a little pickerel hiding in weeds. The best method of catching them is to sweep the net through weed beds and hope you bag one. If you try to dip net a pickerel spotted hovering in open water, the chances are pretty good that you'll miss. They can be incredibly swift when danger threatens!

The smaller pickerels and pikes will do very well in a home aquarium if *plenty* of live foods are provided. Small pickerels can be fed live brine shrimp, tubifex worms, and baby guppies, if you don't mind feeding small fishes to other fishes. As they grow the fish will accept earthworms and bait minnows. But once a pickerel reaches 7 inches, it will eat about four or five small bait minnows a day. Keep that in mind before you bring that little pickerel home! A pickerel *must* have living prey because it does not recognize chopped fish or meat as food and will starve to death if offered this food.

The pickerels' tank should be thickly planted and not too brightly lit.

They will *generally* get along with other fishes close to their own size—in other words, too big to swallow.

# Suckers

Suckers are fairly large fish that look somewhat like trout in body shape but have a very different mouth. The trout's mouth is the strong-jawed mouth of a predator. The sucker's mouth has the thick, fleshy lips of a bottom grazer, a fish that eats plants growing on the bottom. About 60 species of suckers are found in the United States and Canada. Some of them are very common and others are very rare and considered endangered. Some of the more common species are the white sucker, the Sacramento sucker, the lake chubsucker, the hog sucker, and the spotted sucker. Some suckers, such as the various redhorse suckers and the hog sucker, are found mostly in creeks and rivers. But most of the other species are common in lakes and bogs.

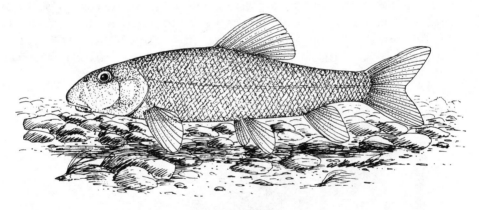

The common, or white, sucker.

The white sucker is typical of the group and has a very wide distribution. Therefore, it can serve as a model for most of the other species. This fish is found over much of the continent, from Alaska and northern Canada south to Texas and Georgia. It has been widely introduced elsewhere so that today there aren't too many rivers and lakes that don't have the white sucker as a resident.

This sucker can get large—up to about 26 inches. Although it is not very colorful, it is an attractive creature. The back may be olive-greenish to black and the sides are goldish or silvery and very shiny. The male becomes quite beautiful when **spawning;** he turns gold all over and has a bright red band along the side and reddish fins. White suckers often "run up" small streams and brooks entering lakes to spawn. They sometimes move upstream in dense schools containing hundreds of fish.

Small suckers can be collected in shallow water where the bottom is sandy. They can be seined when they gather in small schools. Or a baited minnow trap can be placed near weeds underneath a bank overhang. Suckers are very hardy and usually transport without any trouble, seldom requiring any aeration in the fish box.

Suckers will thrive in almost any aquarium setup. They prefer a tank that has at least some algae growth, because these fishes are omnivorous, eating both plant and animal matter. As these fishes are great rooters and grubbers, they may keep the bottom stirred up and the water cloudy if too many are kept in one tank. They are peaceful creatures that will not bother other fishes. They are not picky eaters, accepting nearly all types of the usual fish foods.

# Sunfishes

There are about 20 species of sunfishes in North America. Nearly all of them have been kept in aquariums with great success. The sunfishes probably have more nicknames than any other fish group. In various parts of the country, people call them "bream," "brim," "kivvers," "sun bass," "sun perch," and just plain old "sunnies," among many other names.

The beautiful
black-banded sunfish.

Sunfishes are relatives of the basses, but they are much smaller and less aggressive. They range in size from the tiny pygmy sunfishes, which are mature at about 1½ inches, to the bluegill and pumpkinseed sunfishes, which may reach 16 inches. Crappies, which are also sunfishes, may reach 20 inches.

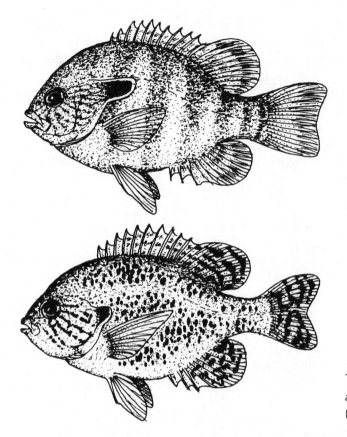

The longear sunfish (top) and pumpkinseed sunfish (bottom).

The sunfishes are found throughout the central and eastern part of North America. Some species also have been introduced into the West and even Hawaii as game fishes. They are found in many different habitats, including rivers, lakes, swamps, bogs, and farm ponds. Most sunfishes prefer habitats with plenty of vegetation and other such shelter. They seldom venture out into deeper water.

Sunfishes have chunky, rounded bodies and spiny dorsal fins. Many species also have a dark **ear flap,** or "ear spot" on the **gill cover.** They are often very brightly colored, especially the males during spawning. Although they may gather in groups wherever they are found, sunfishes do not really live in schools the way shiners and other more sociable fishes do. It's pretty much every fish for itself in sunfish society!

Sunfishes can be collected by virtually every method we've discussed, from the seine net to the minnow trap. They are "smart" fishes, though, and not easily corralled into tight spots where they can be netted. Using a small seine is probably the best way to collect them near sandy bottoms and weed beds.

These fishes make good aquarium inhabitants, and when small, they will get along well with most other fishes. Larger sunfishes can be quite aggressive, however. There will be much chasing about if too many of them are kept in a tank. Always include plenty of rock caves, roots, and large plants in a sunfish tank to allow the fish to set up territories and avoid each other if they want to.

Nearly all sunfishes eagerly accept live foods of all kinds, as well as meat and fish scraps and freeze-dried fish foods. Sunfishes tend to "wash out" and lose their bright colors if they are kept in a brightly lit tank. So keep the lights on the dim side and use black-dyed aquarium gravel you can buy in any pet shop and your sunnies will stay as bright and beautiful as any tropical fish!

# Topminnows

The topminnows, also called killifishes or just plain "minnows," are among the most common and abundant small fishes in North America. The name "killifish" comes from the Dutch word, *kill*, meaning "creek." Smaller, slow-moving creeks are among the best places to look for topminnows!

Lakes and bogs and even roadside ditches are home to many topminnows, which make excellent and hardy aquarium fishes. There are about 40 species of topminnows inhabiting salt, brackish, and fresh waters in North America.

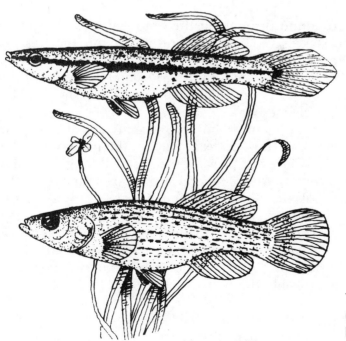

The blackstripe topminnow (top) and the goldear killifish (bottom).

Topminnows get their common name from their habit of swimming at or very close to the water's surface. The **upturned mouth** is located on the top of the fish's snout, allowing it to eat small food items floating on the water. In addition to their habit of swimming near the surface, topminnows and killifishes can be distinguished by their flattened head and back, large eyes, and the dorsal fin located far back on the body. They are brightly colored and easily observed because they rarely swim very deep or inhabit deeper waters far from shore.

Many topminnows can be collected for the aquarium, with more species found in the southern states than in cooler northern areas. Some of the more familiar species are the banded killifish, the northern studfish, the plains topminnow, golden topminnow, the blackstripe topminnow, and the pretty little bluefin killifish that lives in Georgia and Florida. All of these fishes are found in the quieter, weedy places near the shorelines of lakes, rivers, and creeks. There they swim actively about at the surface hunting for insects and other small organisms.

Topminnows are best collected with a dip net because their often muddy, soft-bottomed habitat may make dragging a seine around difficult. Fast action is required to bag them, though. At the first sign of danger, topminnows can dart swiftly out of sight and remain hidden for a long time. The best approach is to sneak up on a feeding school and make a quick, deep sweep of the net in toward the shore, since topminnows tend to dive into shoreline weeds when frightened. Some species can be caught in a minnow trap baited with bread or corn and placed among thick weeds in waters where they have been observed.

The killifish aquarium should have a wide water surface area to give the fish plenty of "cruising" room. The type of setup isn't really important—rocks, plants, and gnarled roots can all be included in the decor. The tank should be securely covered as these fishes are very active and may do some jumping if they are startled.

Topminnows and killifishes are among the easiest native fishes to feed. Being surface feeders, they will eagerly accept all floating foods, including flake foods sold for tropical fishes and goldfishes. They will also eat any live foods and bits of meat or fish.

# Crayfish

Crayfish, or crawfish and crawdads, as they are sometimes called, are often kept as scavengers in aquariums. Many are sold in pet shops under the name "freshwater lobster." This is not really dishonest advertising because the crayfish is a very close relative of the saltwater lobster.

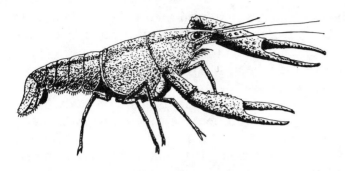

Smaller crayfish can be kept in an aquarium as scavengers. A large one may attack fishes at night.

These small **crustaceans,** are **invertebrates,** or animals with hard skeletons on the *outside* of their bodies. They are found in a wide variety of habitats, from swift streams to lakes to marshes. More species are found in the southern states, where most inhabit small rivers and creeks that are not polluted. The more common species of crayfish are usually a mottled or spotted brownish-reddish-gold color. Sometimes white, bright red, or blue varieties are seen, just as they are in the lobster. Large adults may reach 5 or 6 inches in length.

Crayfish are usually collected by turning over rocks in a stream or at a lake shore and grabbing the crayfish hiding beneath before they have a chance to escape. Like lobsters, crayfish are perfectly capable of defending themselves. They will pinch if they get the chance, but only a very large one can pinch hard enough to hurt.

These crustaceans will live very well in a native fishes aquarium and will scavenge all food leftovers they can find. In this way, they perform a valuable service in the tank—as they do in nature. But don't be fooled into thinking a crayfish will be satisfied with leftovers when it can have fresh fish as well. A larger crayfish will attack and devour fishes at night, when it can surprise them at rest. A small crayfish presents no real danger to larger fishes kept with it. But a big one—say, over 4 inches—may be a real danger. The answer is to collect the smallest crayfish possible—no more than about 2 inches long—and keep them only for as long as it takes them to double in size. Keep an eye on your fishes, and if you discover any missing overnight or having nipped and damaged fins, remove the crayfish at once and release it back into the natural habitat.

Crayfish are highly territorial and will fight among themselves if too many are kept in the same tank. You should limit their number to no more than two (small ones) in a 20-gallon tank. Provide them with rock hideouts so they can set up territories as far from one another as possible. Unless they are badly crowded, crayfish will usually only threaten each other when they meet and then quickly retreat to their caves without actual fighting.

## OTHER WATER CREATURES

Many other smaller creatures live in lakes and bogs and some can be kept in an aquarium. The red-spotted newt, or salamander, aquatic snails, and hundreds of different kinds of water insects often turn up in nets during fish-collecting trips. Snails make good tank scavengers, though they may multiply and become too numerous. Newts can be kept for a while and fed live foods or small earthworms. Aquatic insects can be kept in a small aquarium or jar and observed for a few days. Then you should release them, since they are hard to feed and may be eaten by larger fishes.

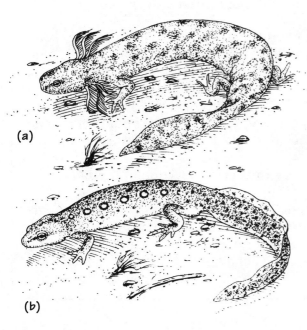

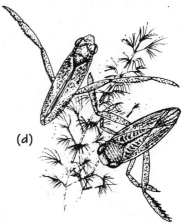

The mudpuppy (a) and the red-spotted newt (b) can both be kept with fishes when they are smaller. Pond snails (c) make excellent tank scavengers as long as they are not too abundant! The water boatman and the backswimmer (d) are common aquatic insects that can be observed in a small container for a while and then released. Be careful to keep the jar covered because these insects can fly!

The fishes we've discussed in this chapter are far from the only kinds that might be found in lakes and bogs. While exploring you may catch goldfish and carp that people have released and have "gone wild." These look just like pet-store fish, except that over time their colors have returned to the dull, bronzy gold of the original wild fishes. Many species of shiners and chubs, as well as such fishes as pike-perches, yellow perch, and sticklebacks, are found in lakes. If you collect a fish that looks odd and you can't identify it, borrow a field guide to fishes at your library and look it up. A good field guide is an excellent investment when you find your interest in the aquatic world growing!

## The Lake and Bog Community Tank

Our lakes and bogs are home to many more predatory fishes than most streams are. Thus you'll have to be careful about what you include in your tank. If you collect lake shiners or mudminnows, don't keep them with pickerels, a young bass, or a bowfin unless these fishes are very small. Even then, keep an eye on the predators. As soon as they begin to grow larger and "eyeball" your other fishes with interest, take them back to the lake or bog where you collected them and release them!

To be on the safe side, try to keep a collection of the same type of fishes, rather than trying to mix predators and prey fishes together, even though they may be small. In other words, a tank full of shiners or small sunfishes (a **single-species tank**) makes a very pretty sight. But an aquarium with a couple of hungry basses or pickerels is really better for the study of predatory behavior in fishes. If you plan your lake aquarium's fish population, you'll have less trouble later on.

# Chapter 6

# Gently Down the Stream

The sight and sound of running water appeals to almost everyone, but rivers are much more than a pretty view. They are also an important part of the planet's **hydrologic cycle.** That is the process by which water, essential to all life on earth, circulates from the atmosphere to the surface of the land and then to the sea, where it is lifted back to the atmosphere again through evaporation. In this way, all living things on earth are supplied with the wonder liquid that makes all organic existence possible.

The streams and rivers in which you observe and collect water life may be very different and go by many names, depending on where you

The stream habitat.

live. There really isn't a typical river or stream, because so many factors affect the way a waterway looks and moves.

Most rivers begin high among hills and in mountains, where they often originate as springs that grow to become narrow **freshets** and tributaries. When the stream levels off and slows down a bit, it may be called a brook, creek, or branch. When a stream or creek becomes large enough for boats to move on it without hitting gravel banks or sand **bars,** it can be called a river. Larger rivers in North America have a great variety of fishes and other water animals. But it can be dangerous trying to collect water animals in deeper rivers, so always stick close to the shoreline, where most of the best aquarium fishes are found anyway!

As with fish collecting in lakes and bogs, always take a friend along when you go collecting. An adult who "knows the ropes" should also accompany you when you explore streams and rivers.

Most big rivers have sheltered coves, **backwaters,** and marshy areas where the water current slows down and there is a lot of vegetation. These are the spots to sweep your net or set your fish trap for aquarium fishes. The gentler the current, such as in a **run,** or **pool,** the easier it is to handle nets and place minnow traps. A strong current makes it difficult to judge distance when netting a fish. Because the fishes are always on the move in flowing water, they can be tough to corral in small areas of the shoreline.

Most of our large rivers usually flow through many cities and towns on their way to the sea and are often quite polluted, especially further downstream. If you live near the river's source, before it flows through any cities, the fish collecting will be better. You can very likely use the river's water to fill your aquarium. Further downstream, however, it will be safer to to use aged tap water rather than risk using river water, even though the fishes came from the river in the first place. This is because the cleanliness of river water can change rapidly and suddenly, especially right after a rain, when many pollutants are washed into the river from the surrounding land.

Most stream fishes eventually become acclimated to the home aquarium as long as the water is cool enough and well aerated. At first they may have a little trouble maintaining their "balance" in the still water of the tank because they've been long accustomed to fighting the stream's current. But within a week or so they will behave as if they were born there!

Flowing rivers of any size are not the only places you can collect wild aquarium fishes. If you live in some of the warmer parts of North America you'll be able to collect fishes and other small water life in some pretty surprising places. Have you ever thought of a roadside ditch or a drainage culvert as a place to look for aquarium fishes? If not, you may be missing an opportunity to stock your tank the easy way!

In many southern states, roadside ditches that are filled with water all year long often have a surprising variety of aquatic wildlife living in or near them. The combination of hot summers and very mild winters makes it possible for small fishes and other creatures to survive very well in narrow ditches that are connected to natural bodies of water. Look for places near bridges or other road crossings because these spots often have more sloping banks and access to the water is easier and safer. When entering the water, always take your time and look before you take a step and wade in!

## SOME STREAM AND RIVER FISHES

# Dace

The name *dace* is often applied to small fishes belonging to several different groups of minnows. All dace, however, are true minnows, like shiners, and most, but not all, dace are found in streams.

Probably the most typical dace are the redbelly, the blacknose, and the speckled dace. Another species, the longnosed dace, is a very common but little-known fish that lives in a very specialized habitat. We'll talk about this fish later on.

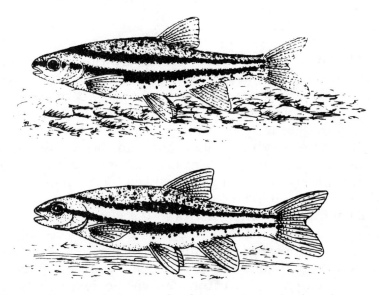

The southern redbelly dace (top) has a darker back and narrower gold stripe than the northern dace (bottom). These dace are among the most colorful of North American fishes.

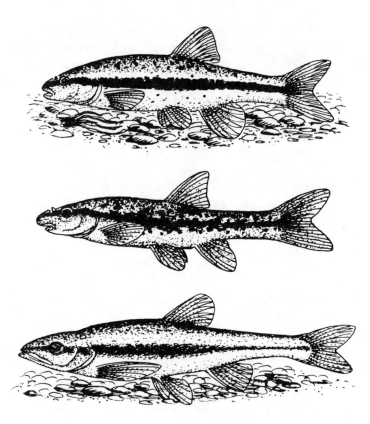

Top to bottom: the blacknose dace, the longnose dace, and the redside dace.

Most dace are small fishes, seldom growing larger than 5 inches. For much of the year they are rather drab creatures. They are mostly brownish or olive-green on the back and silvery or gold below with one or two dark stripes running from nose to tail. But during the spring breeding season the males of many species become very brightly colored.

Dace live in clear, clean streams and smaller rivers throughout the United States and southern Canada. They are vulnerable to water pollution and quickly disappear if their stream is contaminated with sewage or agricultural runoff. The brown and gold longnosed dace is found in fast-flowing streams from Alaska in the west to Quebec in the east and south to Missouri and Georgia. They are usually found hiding beneath rocks in the stream bed. They are often collected by holding a dip net just downstream of a rock and then flipping it over. If there are any dace hiding there they will be carried into the net by the swift current.

Most dace are very swift and agile creatures that are not easily caught unless they can be cornered in a small pocket of the stream. One of the best ways to collect dace is to construct a rock fish trap of the kind described in Chapter 3. This type of fish collecting usually requires the cooperation of two or more people: two to drive the fishes into the trap from upstream and one to be ready with the net at the end of the trap.

All dace are peaceful and hardy and will get along with most other fishes in the aquarium. They will eat most prepared fish foods as well as all types of live foods. Dace should not be kept with such larger predatory fishes as bass, bowfins, or pickerel, which are their natural enemies and would quickly make a meal of them!

# Darters

Darters are among the most abundant small stream fishes, yet they may be the least known, even among trout anglers, who spend more time near streams than most people do! There are about 125 species of darters in

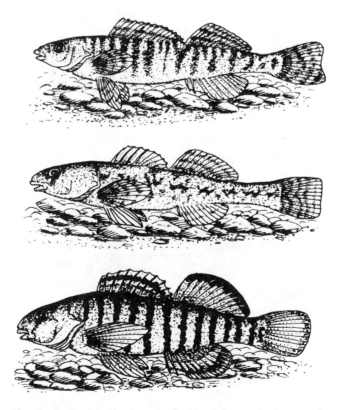

Top to bottom: the logperch, the johnny darter, and the rainbow darter, one of the most colorful native fishes.

the United States. Most of them are found in streams in the southeastern states. They are all small fishes, ranging in size from the 7-inch logperch to the 1½-inch least darter.

The most famous darter of all is the tiny snail darter of Tennessee. This little fish is found in only a couple of small streams in the northeastern part of the state. When one of those streams was threatened by a giant dam, work on the project was halted—at least for a while—in order to save the fish.

The 4-inch Maryland darter has apparently already disappeared forever. This fish was found only in a single **riffle,** or shallow, fast-running part, of one stream in Maryland. None have been seen or collected there for the past five years so the species is believed to be extinct.

Darters are very sensitive to habitat destruction because their shallow, flowing stream habitats are easily contaminated by sewage and agricultural pesticides. Any toxic substance dumped into a stream will be carried by the current and contaminate the waterway for many miles downstream.

In spite of the unhappy future some darters face, many species are still very common and can be collected for the freshwater aquarium. Among these are the johnny, the orangefin, and the rainbow darter. You may also find a couple of species of logperch, which are just larger darters. All darters, by the way, are closely related to the yellow perch and the walleye, both much larger and very popular game fishes.

How can you tell a darter from all of the other small fishes that live in streams? One of the best ways is by watching its behavior. All darters lack the **swim bladder** that most fishes have and that allows them to

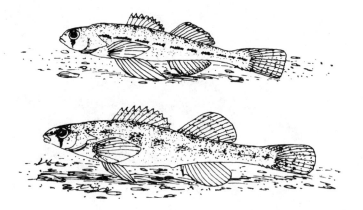

The least darter (top) and the swamp darter (bottom) are two small species that often live in slow-moving streams or even in still water.

Sculpins share the stream habitat with darters but they are more secretive. Compared to darters, sculpins are stubby, big-headed little fishes with large mouths.

move freely about at all levels of the water. The bladder is a small, gas-filled organ that a fish uses to change its **buoyancy** (how much it floats) and move up or down in the water. Darters, lacking the swim bladder, are always heavier than water. Thus they spend nearly all of their time swimming, or "darting," rather jerkily about on the stream bottom. They can, of course, swim upward to grab a bit of food drifting by. But unlike most other fishes that can hover in midwater with ease, a darter sinks back down to the bottom as soon as it stops swimming.

Darters are slender fishes with two dorsal fins and large, fanlike pectoral fins. When they are not in breeding colors, most species are olive-greenish or brown on the top and marked with irregular bands and blotches. When they are seen from above they closely match the color and pattern of the pebbly or sandy stream bottom. A darter is often not noticed until it moves.

These little fishes look similar to sculpins, which inhabit streams as well. Sculpins have larger heads and pectoral fins and spend much of their time hiding beneath rocks on the stream bottom. They can be kept in a well-aerated aquarium and fed live foods.

Both darters and sculpins are fairly easy to collect. They can be caught by hauling a small minnow seine over pebbly or sandy parts of the stream and bringing the net into a shallow cove or indentation in the bank. A minnow trap set among rocks or next to the stream bank will usually turn up a few darters and sculpins if it is left there overnight. Another way to collect these fishes is to use the "rock shuffle" method. One person can do this. It involves holding a dip net against the stream bottom and then shuffling your feet among the rocks just upstream of the net. When the rocks are disturbed, any small fishes hiding underneath them, including darters, will be swept into the net by the current. It's important to lift the net quickly after each "shuffle session" because darters are no fools when they think they are in a trap!

Nearly all darters will get along fine with other smaller stream fishes. They are not difficult to maintain in the aquarium. Ideally, the tank should be no smaller than 20 gallons and the filtration system must be a good one—preferably a canister filter system. Darters prefer cooler, well-aerated water and a substrate that at least resembles a stream bottom. Small to medium-sized pebbles and stones will be fine as a base. Larger rocks and waterlogged roots collected right in the stream can be arranged near the back of the tank to complete the effect. Remember, carefully scrub all rocks and roots before placing them in the tank.

Plants are not necessary in a stream tank, but any you may find growing naturally in the stream, such as *Fontinalis* or *Elodea,* can be collected, rinsed well, and planted toward the rear of the aquarium. Try to place the plants so they are gently moved by the filter's flow. This way silt and debris cannot gather on their leaves.

Although darters and sculpins are peaceful creatures that will get along with other fishes, they are at their best when kept alone in the tank. Kept by themselves and fed a varied diet of live and prepared foods, a number of darter species have spawned in aquariums. If your darters begin to show interest in spawning, disturb them as little as possible and you will see them at their best. It is at this time the males become every bit as colorful as any of the most popular tropical aquarium fishes.

# Fallfish and Creek Chub

The fallfish is best described as a *big* minnow, and that's exactly what it is. It is the largest minnow native to eastern North America. This fish reaches a length of 22 inches. Because it will take a baited hook or even an artificial trout fly, many an inexperienced trout angler has thought he or she had a huge trout on the line when a fallfish grabbed the bait!

This fish is found over most of the eastern United States, where it lives in the deeper parts of streams and smaller rivers. Adult fallfish are, of course, much too large for the average home aquarium. But the young ones make good aquarium fish because they are active and peaceful creatures that are easy to care for. The young fishes gather in small schools among the rocks and weeds in shallow water, where they can be collected with a dip net or a baited minnow trap.

The fallfish is not a brightly colored creature. It is olive-greenish on the back and silvery or yellowish on the sides and belly. During the breeding season in the spring, the male grows large, spiky bumps, or **tubercles,** on the top of his head and his sides shimmer with rainbow colors—about the most colorful he'll ever be.

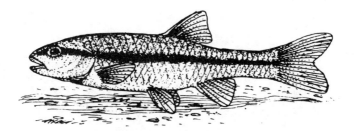

Creek chub, a common stream minnow, reaches a length of about 14 inches. Smaller ones make great aquarium fishes.

The creek chub is a close relative of the fallfish, but it only grows to about half its size and is more colorful. It is a typical large minnow found throughout the eastern part of North America. It also has been widely introduced elsewhere, including rivers and streams in Texas and California.

At most times of the year, the creek chub is plain olive-greenish or brown on the back and silvery on the sides. The young fish up to about 4 inches—the best size for the aquarium—are a reddish brown on the back and silvery white below with a dark brown or black stripe down the side. When males are in spawning condition, they are very colorful, with orange lower fins, bright blue on the side of the head, and rosy tints on the sides. During spawning, males dig a long pit in the gravel of the stream bed and lure the females into the nest. These nests may be 6 feet long and 1 foot high and look like long ridges of sand or gravel in the stream bottom. Other fishes, such as shiners and dace, may also lay their eggs in the creek chub's nest for the extra protection it gives their own eggs and young.

Both of these fishes can be kept with all other peaceful stream fishes when they are small. When they grow larger than about 6 inches they can become aggressive. They will eat all the usual fish foods, and they especially like earthworms and tubifex worms. As with any species of native fishes that grow much larger when they are adults, fallfish should be kept and enjoyed in a tank for a year or two and then released back into the wild before they become a problem.

# Madtom Catfishes

The madtoms are a group of small catfishes that live primarily in flowing streams or brooks. They are very secretive and can be hard to find because they hide beneath the rocks and debris on the bottom. The largest madtom is the tadpole madtom, which grows to a length of about 8 inches. This

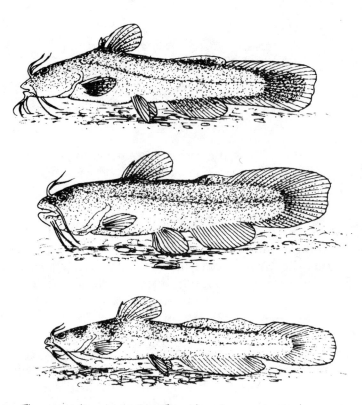

Three madtom species. Top: the stonecat reaches a
length of about 12 inches and is the largest
madtom in North America. Center: the tadpole
madtom. Bottom: the slender madtom.

catfish is found throughout most of the eastern United States where it
lives in lakes and bogs in addition to streams and rivers. The stonecat is
another larger madtom. This fish grows to about 6 inches and is common
in smaller lakes. But people may not even know it is there because of its
secretive habits. Most of the other madtoms are small, seldom growing
larger than 4 or 5 inches. Some species living in the southeastern states,
such as the tiny smoky and scioto madtoms, are quite rare and are
considered endangered. This unhappy situation is due to the destruction
or pollution of their stream habitats and the fact that many small rivers
have been dammed or "cleaned up" by being channelized.

The smaller madtoms make excellent aquarium fishes. You can collect them by placing a minnow trap baited with a chicken neck among the
rocks of the stream or lake and leaving it there overnight. Or you can
simply turn over rocks and logs and scoop up the fish as they try to escape.
You'll have to move fast, though. Although a madtom looks sluggish, it
can move quickly if it has to.

Madtoms should be kept in an aquarium that has plenty of hiding places. Larger rocks and stones, as well as pieces of bogwood and roots, should be part of the tank's decorations. Keep the light on the dim side because these shy fishes will remain in hiding all the time if the lights are bright!

Madtoms will eat virtually anything that most other fishes will. They favor live foods, pieces of raw meat or fish, and earthworms. If they are well cared for, madtom catfishes will live for at least ten years in an aquarium.

# Shiners

The name *shiner* can be confusing, just as the name *minnow* can be. Just what is a shiner or a minnow? Many people believe that *any* small fish is

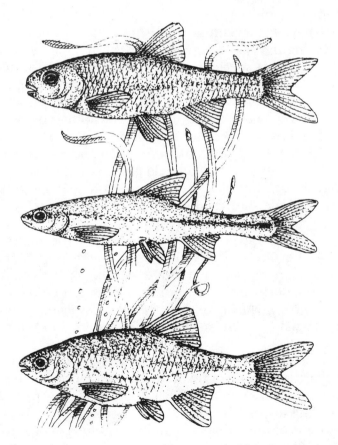

Top to bottom: common shiner, weed shiner, and red shiner.

a minnow and that any small, *silvery* fish is a shiner. They're partly right and partly wrong.

*Shiner* is not a scientific name, but *minnow* is, even though it sounds like a common name, or nickname. The word *shiner* is usually applied to small fishes, or minnows found in lakes or streams. Minnows are members of the fish family *Cyprinidae*, which is the largest fish group in the world. There are more than 2,100 species of minnows. They are found on all the continents of the world except Antarctica, Australia, and South America. The United States and Canada have more than 230 different species of minnows. They vary in size from the tiny, 3-inch weed shiner to the introduced carp, which may reach 48 inches in length and weigh up to 10 pounds!

About 125 species of fishes are actually called shiners in North America. Some of the more abundant shiners are the common shiner, the silverfin shiner, the weed shiner, and the emerald shiner. Most are less than 6 inches long, and the majority of them live in streams or rivers. At most times of the year, many of the shiners can be hard to tell apart because they are all plain silvery fishes with dark stripes or bands on their sides. During the spawning season in spring and early summer, though, the males of most species become extremely brilliant in coloration. They are just as bright and beautiful as many of the most popular tropical fishes.

One of the best ways to determine which species of shiner you have caught is to get a good field guide and consult it when you bring your fish home. The Peterson *Field Guide to Freshwater Fishes* (Boston: Houghton Mifflin, 1991) is one of the better guidebooks to our native fishes and is highly recommended. A good field guide will help you identify *any* fishes you may collect, not only the very confusing shiner group!

Of all of the shiners, the common shiner is one of the larger species. This fish grows to a length of about 7 inches and is greenish-brown on the back and bright silver on the sides. When the males are in breeding condition they are very beautiful, with bright reddish or rosy tints on the sides and fins. This shiner is found in cool, clear rivers and streams over much of the northeastern part of the country. It has several close relatives in other parts of North America. Many are so similar that only a trained **ichthyologist,** a scientist who studies fishes, can tell the difference between them!

The smaller weed, or bridle, shiners are probably the most difficult to tell apart. Nearly all of them are slim little fishes that are darkish above and silvery below, with a blackish or dark brown stripe along the sides. In the breeding season, the male shiners become quite spectacular, taking on all the colors of the rainbow, with brilliant reds, blues, and yellows tinting the fishes' sides and bellies.

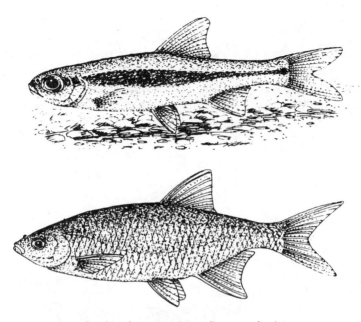

Spotfin (top) and golden (bottom) shiners.

The golden shiner is one of the larger shiners, reaching a length of about 13 inches when full grown. This fish originally was found only in the eastern half of North America. But it is so popular as a bait fish that it has been transplanted far and wide, even to lakes and streams in the Far West. The golden shiner is one of the few shiners that actually gets large enough to be caught on a hook and line. It is a beautiful, brassy-golden fish that does very well in the aquarium.

Some shiners, such as the golden shiner and the slim little emerald shiner, are found in large lakes as well as in swift-flowing streams, but they quickly adapt to the standing water of an aquarium. Shiners should be kept in as large a tank as possible because they are active, schooling fishes that need plenty of room to move about. If you keep shiners, avoid keeping just one or two, for these fishes are much happier when they have lots of their own kind for company. In a 20-gallon tank, you can keep 6 to 10 shiners if you avoid crowding the tank with a lot of decorations. A sandy or pebbly substrate and a root and tall plants toward the back of the tank are all you really need in an aquarium housing shiners.

These active and attractive fishes can be fed a wide variety of fish foods. In general, shiners will eat everything that most tropical fishes will—from live foods to the flakes and pellets sold in pet shops. Be sure not to overfeed in a shiner tank, however. These fishes will quickly feel the effects of a polluted tank!

# Stream Suckers

There are 63 species of suckers found in North America. Most of them are medium-sized to large fishes that look like big minnows. Many suckers live in lakes and some, like the white sucker, live in both lakes and streams. A few species are found only in streams; these are the so-called redhorses and one strange-looking fish called the hog sucker.

The odd-looking hogsucker is one of the more common suckers in streams throughout eastern North America.

Nearly all suckers are hardy creatures that adapt very well to the aquarium and will live for a long time if they're fed adequately. Some of the larger suckers may hang around for 30 or 40 years—much too long if you're thinking of putting something else in your tank as a change!

Suckers can be distinguished from the minnows and other similar fishes by their larger scales, their rather stocky and solid bodies, and their blunt, rounded heads with the thick-lipped mouth on the underside. This type of mouth clearly indicates a fish that feeds almost exclusively on the bottom. The sucker's eyes are placed rather high on its head and are fairly small for the size of the fish. The overall effect is a sort of wide-eyed, dopey expression that is quite different from most other fishes.

Suckers may look dumb but they are well adapted to their environment. They are not at all easy to catch, at least with a net. Although they spend much of their time prowling slowly over the stream's bottom picking up bits of food, they are quite aware of what's going on around them and can move fast when they have to. The best method of catching them for the aquarium is the seine. Since smaller suckers usually move about in shallow water near the stream's edge, it's generally not difficult to surround them with the net and herd them up against the bank. Suckers will also enter a minnow trap baited with bread and set among rocks in quieter parts of the stream.

Suckers are very peaceful creatures, and even a larger one will not bother other fishes in the same tank. The filtration in a sucker tank, however, should be relatively powerful and efficient. These fishes love to root about in the sand and will keep the water cloudy in a tank that has only a small corner filter setup.

Suckers will eat almost any fish foods, from earthworms and pieces of fish to nearly any prepared pet shop foods. They will also eat any algae that is growing in the tank. These fish make great scavengers—there is little leftover food that they will miss in their endless rooting and grubbing.

## OTHER WATER CREATURES

# Tadpoles and Frogs

A tadpole is basically what a **larva** is to an adult insect—it is the immature stage of a frog or toad. Both tadpoles and adult frogs may be found in or near a wide variety of aquatic habitats, from marshes and bogs to rivers and large lakes. These small amphibians have many enemies that would

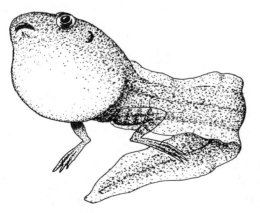

Frog tadpoles have a huge appetite for green foods and will eat any algae or live plants in the aquarium.

readily make a meal of them. Therefore, they are always found near the shoreline and as close to protective vegetation as possible. The word *amphibian* comes from the Latin and is the combination of two words: *amphi,* meaning "two," and *bios,* which means "life." Thus a frog or toad lives two lives: one as a tadpole living in water and the other as an adult that can leave the water and live on land.

Amphibians in general and frogs in particular have become much less common over the past 20 years. Habitat destruction by urban and suburban development is one cause of amphibian decline. But the real causes, such as the effect of acid rain on these water creatures, may be much harder to correct.

Because amphibians are in some trouble in North America, it's not a good idea to collect any and remove them from the habitat unless you can see that they are very common where you are fish collecting. Even then, it's a good idea to make keeping and observing these animals a temporary project and to release them back into the natural habitat in early fall.

Tadpoles are usually found in warmer, shallow water near the shoreline of rivers and lakes. They can move swiftly when danger threatens, but generally they are easy to collect with a dip net or seine. Aquarists often catch tadpoles accidentally, as they simply turn up in the net during fish-collecting activities. Frog tadpoles are usually much larger than toad tadpoles, which may be as small as a half an inch and very dark, almost black in color. Green frog and bullfrog tadpoles are large and are usually mottled olive-greenish with lighter colored bellies. They are often found on the bottom in more open water as well as in weed beds.

Most tadpoles are hardy creatures and can tolerate poor water conditions much better than fishes can. Healthy tadpoles may even be observed in small warm pools of water that are drying up in late summer, which shows that they can survive as long as there is any water at all. This is because these animals can take oxygen directly from the air with specialized breathing organs, something very few fishes can do. In the aquarium, a tadpole will frequently dart to the surface, gulp a bubble of air, and dash down again.

If your aquarium has plenty of live plants, a thick algae growth on the glass, and some natural debris on the bottom, the tadpoles will need very little food. They will graze on the plants and rummage through the bottom material. If the tank has plastic plants or is a "clean" one, the "polliwogs" will have to be fed. They can be offered spinach or mustard leaves that have been lightly boiled to soften them. Avoid feeding them lettuce leaves as this plant has very low nutritional value.

Adult frogs are not a good idea for the average aquarium setup as they often escape from most tanks and end up scampering around the house or drying up in room corners!

# River Turtles

Aquatic turtles are usually found in or near a river, lake, or marsh. The larger adult turtles are too big to be kept in most home aquariums, but young ones can be very appealing little creatures. Nearly all species will do well in the aquarium. The only trouble with turtles is that most species will catch and eat fish if they get the chance. While this fish-eating habit may not be much of a problem if the turtle is very small and the fishes in the tank are large and quick enough to stay out of its way, the tables will be turned when the turtle grows. For this reason, it's usually best to keep small turtles in the same type of terrarium used to keep frogs and toads.

Many species of turtles are found in rivers and streams. They are usually easily collected, either with a dip net or by hand, if they are spotted in shallow water. Most adult river turtles spend a lot of time basking on logs and rocks some distance from shore. Because they usually drop into the water at the first sign of danger, they cannot be caught easily.

Some of the turtle species you're likely to encounter during a day's fish collecting on rivers and streams include the painted, map, musk, mud, and softshell turtles, as well as the snapping turtle. Of these, only the first four can be safely kept with fishes, and only when small. Both the snapper and the softshell turtle will stalk and attack fishes of any size, especially at night when the fishes are not active. So if you wish to keep a young snapping turtle or a softshell, give it a small tank all to itself!

Baby musk and mud turtles make good aquarium tenants, especially when they are very small. A newly hatched musk turtle is about the size of a nickel and is extremely cute—as turtles go. They are blackish or brownish in color and very easy to miss in the net because they look like tiny lumps of mud or small nuts. In the wild, these turtles are almost entirely aquatic and seldom leave the water. In the aquarium, they spend

The musk turtle, or stinkpot, makes a good aquarium animal when small. Adults will chase and attack fishes and should not be kept in community tanks!

much of their time prowling about looking for food and peering near-sightedly through the glass at the goings-on outside the tank.

Little musk and mud turtles quickly lose their fear of people after adapting to aquarium life. They will readily approach you to be fed. They are almost entirely carnivorous and will accept bits of meat or fish, as well as earthworms. These turtles will also eagerly eat snails, so don't include snails in a musk or mud turtle tank, except as food for the turtle!

All aquatic turtles, except for the snapping turtle, appreciate at least some floating plants in their tank so they can rest at the surface of the water. The snapper only comes to the surface to breathe and returns quickly to the bottom where it resumes its slow prowling about.

In any aquarium that contains both fishes and a turtle or two, the turtles should be fed separately. This is because the active fishes will snatch the bits of food before the slower moving turtles have a chance to get to it. Since most wild turtles tame very quickly, it's often best to feed them by hand or with tweezers—a more enjoyable way to relate to them, anyway!

The best way to keep any wild water turtles collected in early summer is to observe and enjoy them for the warmer months. Then let them go in the natural habitat in the early fall, before temperatures get too low for them to be safely released.

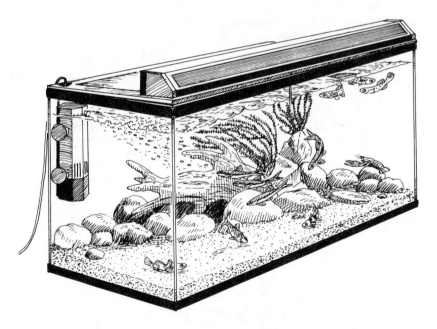

A typical stream aquarium. This tank has an inside canister filter that provides a current for the fishes to swim against. Note that there are few plants in this setup.

A typical terrarium for frogs and small turtles. Flat rocks can be used as a "beach" to separate the soil of the land part of the terrarium from the swimming area.

## The Stream Community Tank

When collecting fishes in rivers and streams, remember that they will have to live together in a container that is much smaller than their native home. To be safe, it's best to keep fishes that are all about the same size. Also, stick to fishes that don't prey upon one another in the wild. This means that you can certainly keep a group of dace and small shiners together. But don't include a bass or small trout if you should happen to catch one. Keep it in another tank, just to be safe! If you collect a few crayfish, keep only one for your tank, and make it the smallest one you have in your bucket! Provide plenty of rock and root hiding places for your stream fishes, and you should have very few problems with fishy squabbling!

# Chapter 7

# Aquarium Activities

Okay, you've got your tank set up. You've collected the fishes and the plants, acclimated them, and they seem to be doing fine. The aquarium looks great. It's clear and clean and fits well in the room. So what's next? What can you do with a home aquarium besides keep it clean, feed the fishes, and just enjoy it?

For many aquarium owners, watching the fishes and "relating" to them by feeding and caring for them is enough reward for the work of setting up the tank and keeping it in good condition. There's nothing wrong with this because aquarium-keeping is *intended* to be a pleasant, uncomplicated activity. But a home aquarium can also offer a fascinating look at the workings of the natural world that few other kinds of pet-keeping can.

Most small animal pets kept in cages cannot behave in all of the complex ways their wild relatives do. But fishes and other small aquatic life may behave exactly as they did in the wild, especially if the tank's setup provides most of the conditions found in nature. If you've taken the time to arrange your native fish aquarium's decorations so that they resemble the fishes' natural habitat as closely as possible, your fishes will feel right at home there. They will soon begin to act as though they were still in their home lake or stream environments.

Basically, activities you can do with your aquarium take two forms. The first is projects that are "passive," or involve simple observations of the behavior of the fishes and other water life. The second is those that are "active," meaning that you may have to make changes in the aquarium's setup or in the way you care for the fishes in order to carry out the experiments.

Let's discuss a few passive observations first.

## Passive Observations

### 1. Making an Observation Cover

Although you can observe the actions of aquarium fishes simply by sitting still in front of the tank, there are drawbacks to this method. Fishes, like people, tend to be less relaxed and less likely to act naturally when they know they are being watched.

While fishes in an aquarium will carry out many of their normal activities in spite of the nearness of people, shy fishes will spend much of their time in hiding, and "pet" fishes will swim right at the front of the tank begging to be fed. Neither of these types of behavior are natural actions. They are the fishes' reactions to people, either as threats or as care-givers.

In order to give aquarium fishes a feeling of complete privacy, you can make a simple observation cover for your tank. In its very simplest form, an observation cover consists of sheets of brown wrapping paper cut to the size of the tank and taped to its front and sides. The front sheet should have a narrow slot about an inch wide running across the tank from side to side. This slot will allow you to quietly peer into the tank without being noticed by the fishes, especially if the surrounding room is darkened.

A paper cover will become torn and ragged after it has been taped up and taken down time after time, so a more sturdy cover made of cardboard is a better idea if you plan to do a lot of fish-behavior studies. This cover can be constructed either of corrugated cardboard or heavy posterboard and lightly taped to the tank's front and sides. The cover should be left in place for as long as you plan to observe your fishes, even over a period of several days or weeks. The privacy offered by a cover may encourage some wild fish species to spawn in an aquarium, which would never happen if they were disturbed by people constantly passing by the tank!

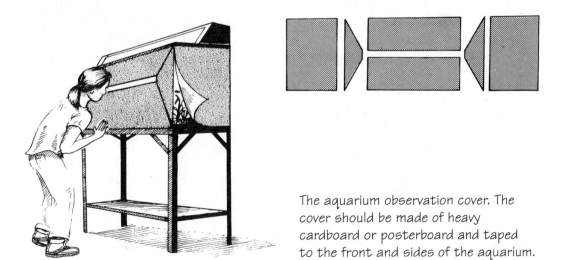

The aquarium observation cover. The cover should be made of heavy cardboard or posterboard and taped to the front and sides of the aquarium.

## 2. Body Shapes

The shape of a fish's body tells a lot about how it behaves and secures its food. Most fishes are grouped under six different behavior types: the rover-predators, the ambush predators, surface-swimming fishes, bottom-living fishes, deep-bodied fishes, and eel-like fishes.

The **rover-predators** have pointed heads and tapered, streamlined bodies that make swimming swiftly through open water easier. This is the "typical" fish shape most people think of when they hear the word *fish*. The minnows, trout, and tunas are typical rover-predators.

The ambush predators have long torpedolike bodies, pointed heads, and fairly large tails. These make fast dashes after passing prey possible. These fishes quietly lie in wait until a smaller fish passes by and then dart out and catch it. Pikes, pickerels, and barracuda are among the ambush predators.

**Surface swimmers** have flattened heads with the mouth located on the upper sides of the snout. This makes it possible for the surface fishes to cruise about and snatch insects and other small prey from the water's surface. The killifishes are typical surface swimmers.

**Bottom fishes** have a wide variety of body shapes, but all of them are adapted to life on or near the bottom. None of the bottom fishes have streamlined bodies because their lifestyle does not involve long periods of active swimming. Catfishes live near the bottom and have large, flattened heads surrounded by slender, sensitive barbels. Flounders and other flatfishes have pancake-thin bodies with the eyes on either the right or left side, so these fishes are always lying on their sides on mud or sand bottoms. Carp and suckers are stout-bodied fishes that have **subterminal mouths** located on the underside of their heads. They use them for rooting and grubbing food items from the sandy or muddy bottom. Darters and sculpins have no swim bladders. Therefore, they are heavier than water and live among the rocks and roots of their stream habitats.

The **deep-bodied fishes** are flattened from top to bottom, making it easy for them to maneuver about in tight places. The butterflyfishes and angelfishes of the coral reefs—as well as the freshwater sunfishes—are typical of this type of fish.

The **eel-like fishes** look something like snakes and usually move about with snaky, swimming motions. These fishes also behave like snakes, preferring habitats that provide them with plenty of hiding places. They thread their way among rocks and roots the way a snake does on land. Morays and the common eel are examples of this type of fish.

Careful observation of your fishes will reveal whether you have one, two, or all of the main fish body types in your tank. Note the type of body form a fish has, and then see if it acts according to the behavior descriptions given here.

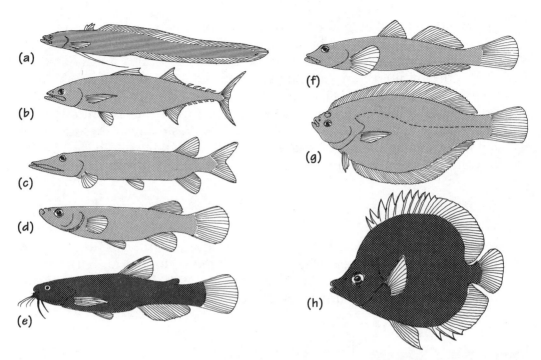

Fish body shapes: (a) eel-like fish, (b) rover-predator,
(c) ambush predator, (d) surface swimmer, (e) bottom prowler,
(f) bottom hugger, (g) flat-bodied fish, (h) deep-bodied fish.

## 3. Scales

The kind of scales a fish has, or whether it has any scales at all, will tell
you a great deal about its lifestyle. Scales are the protective covering of a
fish's body. Their size is a good indication of where the fish lives and how
it behaves. Fishes that are fast swimmers or that live in swiftly flowing
waters usually have smaller scales that feel smooth to the touch. These
small scales, which cover the bodies of trout and tunas, offer less resis-
tance when the fish moves through the water. Fishes that are slow
swimmers or that live in still waters often have larger scales. Carp, suckers, and sunfishes are examples of this kind of fish.

Some bottom fishes also lack scales. Catfishes and eels, which normally live near the bottom and hide in tight places, have either very small
scales or lack them altogether. Their skins feel very smooth and slippery
to the touch.

Other fishes have scales that have been modified into plates or
spines. Nearly all of these fishes are slow movers that hide among aquatic
plants or are camouflaged against the bottom. Pipefishes and seahorses
are peaceful, slow-moving creatures whose bodies are covered by bony

plates. Stingrays, skates, and blowfishes are typical examples of those slow movers that are protected by spiny skins.

The condition of your fishes' scales will tell you a lot about their health. If you notice any missing scales or damaged skin on a fish, keep an eye on it for any possible illness or injury. If whitish fungus develops on the fish or it stops eating, remove the fish from the community tank and place it in a small quarantine container. Freshwater fishes are often helped by adding about a teaspoonful of *noniodized* table salt to each gallon of water and keeping the fish in this mixture for about two days.

## 4. Tails

The shape of a fish's tail, or caudal fin, is closely related to its method of swimming and how fast it moves through the water. Fishes that are on the move in open water usually have curved or forked tails. The more active the fish, the deeper the tail's fork will be. **Pelagic,** or open-water rovers such as tunas and mackerels have sickle-shaped tails that provide

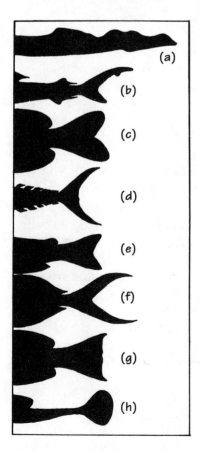

Fish tails: (a) Eel (snake-like swimmer); (b) cruiser (shark); (c) short but fast trips (bass); (d) long-distance speedster (mackerel); (e) bottom burrower (stargazer); (f) agile speedster (jack); (g) slow but steady swimmer (croaker); (h) shy stay-at-home (pipefish).

powerful swimming thrust. Stream fishes such as trouts and minnows that must swim against strong currents have deeply forked tails. Slower-moving fishes or those that spend a lot of time hiding among plants or in crevices usually have squared-off or rounded tails. Most of the catfishes, the flounders, and the killifishes are examples of slow movers with rounded tails.

The tails of the eel-like fishes are rounded, and they may also be connected to the fish's dorsal and **anal fins** in one, continuous fin that runs the entire length of the fish's body. This type of fin design makes it possible for these fishes to swim in the fast, snakelike motion they are known for.

If you've got a combination of shiners, darters, and a small catfish or two in your aquarium, you'll be able to observe how the owners of both forked and rounded tails use them in their daily activities.

## 5. Colors

The colors of your fishes are among the most readily observed and studied aspects of the aquarium. The colors of fishes, like those of nearly all other wild creatures, serve an important purpose in the creature's life. The distinctive appearance of a fish may help it recognize and be recognized by another of its own kind. Or, more importantly, it may help it avoid being eaten by a predator.

The colors and patterns of most fishes are arranged in two ways. The first way makes the fish difficult to see from above or below. And the second closely resembles the fish's surrounding habitat. If you've set up your aquarium with plants and natural gravel so that it looks like the natural aquatic environment, you can easily observe how the fishes' colors and patterns help protect them.

Most animals, including fishes, are darker colored above and lighter below. You can observe this in many creatures, including yourself. The upper side of your arm is almost always darker than its underside, especially when you get a summer tan. This is called **countershading.** It means that an object is colored counter to, or opposite, the natural light from the sun, which creates light above and dark below. Countershading may not be important for humans, but it works very well for fishes. Fishes that swim in open water may be attacked from above by fish-eating birds or from below by larger fishes. You can observe how countershading protects fishes from predators by removing the aquarium cover and looking down into the tank. The fishes are readily visible when you look at them through the aquarium's glass. But they almost disappear against the darker, sand bottom when you look from above. If the water is rippled by the filter's flow, they will be even harder to spot!

To see how a fish's lighter underside protects it, place the fish in a small clear plastic container and hold the container up against a light or the bright sky. Now look up at the fish through the bottom of the container. Although you can see the fish because it is in such a small container, its pale outline looks more like a faint shadow than a solid fish!

Dark bars, blotches, and bands help camouflage the outline of a fish's body and make it almost invisible when the fish is hiding among plants or rocks. If your tank is thickly planted, you may have trouble locating some of your fishes until they move! This is called **protective coloration.** Many wild creatures depend on this natural defense for their survival in a world full of predators!

Some fishes, such as dace and shiners, have a dark stripe running the length of the body from nose to tail. This marking is very noticeable when the fish is observed in an aquarium. But in a lake or stream where a school of fish is moving quickly about in rippled and sunny water, the stripes "break up" the outline of each fish's body. This confuses predators that are seeking to grab a single fish.

While the color patterns of native fishes serve them well in the natural environment, in an aquarium that has only sand and a few decorations they may be very conspicuous. For this reason, always try to decorate your tank so the fishes that will live in it feel at home—even if it means that they can hide and remain out of sight when they want to! Native fishes kept in an aquarium that makes them feel secure will very often change colors when spawning time arrives in the spring. At this time, many species will become much more brightly colored than they are during the other seasons of the year.

## 6. Eyes

An animal's eyes are often the most noticeable parts of its body. They are the organs through which all creatures, including people, view the world around them and react to what they see. We speak of "making eye contact," which tells us how important our eyes are as methods of communication. Most animals will look at another animal's eyes, whether they are friendly toward it or planning to attack it.

The eyes of fishes are similar to our eyes and nearly as complex. Most fishes can see colors and can pick out details in nearby objects. This ability is important when a fish is seeking small prey animals hidden in plants or among debris on the bottom. The lens of the fish's eye is specially adapted to seeing clearly underwater and to giving the fish a wide **field of view,** or area which it can see. Most fishes can see both directly in front and in back of their bodies.

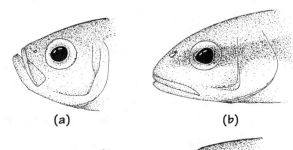

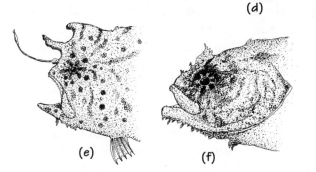

Some fish eyes are more noticeable than others: (a) bigeye, (b) shiner, (c) dace, (d) triggerfish, (e) anglerfish, (f) toadfish.

Fish eyes differ from ours mostly in that they lack eyelids. Since a fish lives in a liquid environment, eyelids and the tear ducts that keep a land animal's eyes moist and protected are not needed. This lack of eyelids gives the fish's eye a "staring" look. Most people think, incorrectly, that a fish has no feelings because we usually determine how another creature feels by looking at its eyes and its facial expression.

When you observe the fishes in your aquarium, you'll notice that your gaze is naturally drawn to each fish's eyes. Since the fishes are "studying" you through the glass in return, it's natural that both creatures—human and fish—tend to concentrate on the eyes of the other when having any contact. The fishes are as aware of what you are doing as you are of their activities.

While you're observing your fishes, take note of the differences in the eyes of the various individuals. In some fishes, the eyes stand out on the fish's head—big and round and very noticeable. Most active fishes that swim in open water have eyes that are not camouflaged in any way. Or they may only be crossed by a single stripe or bar of a darker color. Fishes that live on or near the bottom, or that hide among plants, have eyes that are disguised by dark spots, wavy lines, or even small tabs of flesh around them. These fishes depend on camouflage to hide from enemies or to wait for small prey animals to pass by. So it is important that their eyes cannot be seen and serve as giveaway of their hiding place.

The study of your fishes' eyes will tell you a great deal about how they live and find their food!

## 7. Swimming Behavior

Most fishes swim by flexing their bodies back and forth in a graceful motion. They move slowly when they are at ease and very quickly when they are alarmed or fleeing a predator. Some of the more familiar fishes, such as shiners, basses, and sunfishes, swim this way because they have the long, streamlined shape of the typical fish. Other fishes move about in different ways. Eels use a snakelike motion. Flounders and other flatfishes may glide just above the bottom, flexing their bodies in an up-and-down motion. Darters and sculpins simply hop along on the stream bottom. These fishes do not have swim bladders that help make them buoyant and able to swim in open water.

Some fishes do not use their bodies at all when swimming. Sea-horses, puffers, and triggerfishes vibrate their tails or dorsal and anal fins, moving smoothly along with little or no movement of their bodies. Still other fishes, such as tunas and mackerels, keep their bodies straight but wave their tails in a powerful, back-and-forth movement. That movement

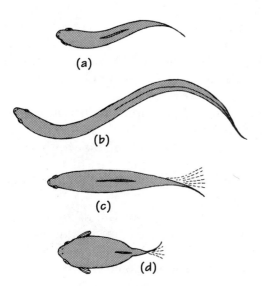

(a)

(b)

(c)

(d)

How fishes swim: (a) "typical" fish motion (shiner); (b) snakelike swimming (eel); (c) using tail only in long-distance swimming (tuna); (d) slow paddling with tail (puffer).

pushes them through the open seas at high speeds—up to 35 miles per hour in large tunas! And, a few fishes hardly ever swim at all! Lumpfishes and the odd little clingfishes spend most of their lives hanging onto rocks and plants. They never move unless they must leave their perch to grab a bit of food.

The swimming behavior of all fishes is geared to their lifestyles. Fishes that poke about in the mud on the bottom or among plants and rocks for their food don't need to swim a great deal. Thus, their bodies and fins are not designed for fast, long-distance swimming. Darters look for tiny animals hiding among the rocks of the stream bottom. The small, hopping motions they make allow them to inspect every nook and cranny of their habitat very closely. Minnows, mackerels, and trout catch their food in open or swiftly flowing water. Their streamlined bodies and broad, powerful fins allow them to move fast over wide areas.

Study the fishes in your tank and note their different swimming behaviors. Compare the little darters, which move on the bottom only when they see food, with the shiners and dace, which are always on the move. You'll see that the longer and more streamlined a fish's body is, the more likely it will be an open-water swimmer always on the go. Fishes that have short, squat bodies or smaller fins tend to be slow-movers that spend a lot of time hiding and waiting for food to come to them.

## 8. Feeding Time

Fishes locate food by sight, smell, and touch. Most open-water, predatory fishes—and these include small fishes such as shiners—simply spot a prey animal and dash up and grab it. Bottom-feeding predators may ambush their prey or sneak up on it. Catfishes have sensitive barbels that "feel" an object on the bottom and let the fish know whether the item is edible. Sharks, piranhas, and bluefish can "smell" blood or body fluids in the water and follow the scent to the source. One way or the other, all fishes are adapted to find food according to their needs and the kind of habitat they live in.

Feeding behavior is one of the easiest behaviors to observe in an aquarium. It can be as simple as dropping flakes or pellets into the tank and watching to see which fishes get to them first. Or you can conduct experiments that take a little more work on the fishes' part. When you've fed your fishes, you've no doubt watched as more active fishes snatched all of the food slowly sinking in the water, while other, slower fishes were left out of the action. Catfishes and other bottom dwellers are often aware that the food is there; it just takes them more time to find it. To demonstrate how quickly hungry fishes notice that something to eat is in their aquarium—even if they can't see it—place about a teaspoonful of meat juice or beef broth in the water near the filter's outflow and watch what happens. As the "scent" of the meat spreads throughout the aquarium, all of the fishes will become much more active and excited. Even sluggish catfishes hidden out of sight among the plants or rocks will emerge and begin swimming eagerly back and forth, seeking the source of that delicious "smell."

## 9. Bad Guys and Good Guys

In general, people think of predators as the "bad guys" of the natural world, and creatures that eat plants as the "good guys." This is because we regard the act of killing another creature as basically "wrong" (even though many of us enjoy eating a juicy hamburger!). The cutting and using of trees and food plants is considered basically "right," or at least excusable, because plants do not have the degree of sensitivity and awareness that animals do.

In nature, there is no such thing as an animal's being "right" or "wrong" in whatever it does to ensure its own survival. There is a place for both predators and plant eaters in the healthy environment, because both help to keep the habitat in its proper balance. Neither group of animals can survive without the other.

This natural cycle can be observed even in the small environment of the aquarium if the tank contains both fishes and living plants. If there are no animals that eat plants in an aquarium, both decorative plants and algae, which are tiny, primitive plants, will grow until they fill the tank and cover the glass and decorations. In this case, the plants become the "bad guys" because they completely overwhelm their environment and leave no room for other organisms.

Snails, tadpoles, and algae-eating fishes are among those creatures that eat plants. When a few of these animals are placed in an algae-covered aquarium, they soon nibble the greenery back to a more desirable level! But, if snails rapidly breed so that there are many of them in a tank, they will become the "bad guys." They will devour nearly all of the plants and create an aquatic "desert." Then, fishes that eat snails, such as sunfishes, have to be introduced into the aquarium to reduce the number of snails. These predators thus become the "good guys"!

You can experiment with the "balance of nature" in an aquarium by setting up a small tank—perhaps a goldfish bowl or a 2-gallon aquarium—and stocking it with plants only. Place the tank in a window so that algae blooms thickly, and then introduce a few snails or a small tadpole to control the algae "weeds." Note how long it takes for the algae eaters to clear up the aquarium. Then observe how quickly the snails multiply until there are too many of them.

# Active Observations

## 1. Breeding Native Fishes

Most native freshwater fishes will not breed in a home aquarium unless the tank is a large one and its conditions are very similar to those found in the natural habitat. Many of our wild fishes spawn only after going through a period of winter inactivity. Since an aquarium is normally kept at room temperature—about 72 degrees—all year long, they do not get the "springtime boost" required to trigger spawning activity.

This doesn't mean, however, that you can't try raising those native freshwater species whose breeding requirements are easy to meet. These "easy breeders" are mostly **live-bearing fishes,** that is, they give birth to living young rather than laying eggs that must be protected from hungry

A live-bearing fish giving birth to its well developed fry. Baby live-bearers can take care of themselves almost immediately after they are born.

fishes (often including the parents) until they hatch. The tropical live-bearers include such old aquarium favorites as guppies, platies, and sword-tails, which will breed readily in a home aquarium. Among the North American live-bearers you can raise in your aquarium are the mosquitofish, the sailfin molly, and the least killifish.

These live-bearers, like tropical guppies and platies, will breed in your aquarium as long as there are plenty of plants for the young fish, or **fry,** to hide in. Ideally, whenever you try to breed *any* fishes, native or tropical, they should be kept in a tank by themselves, not in a community aquarium with many other fishes. They will breed as long as both males and females are present and the water conditions are good. The water should be clean and well filtered. The temperature should be kept at the same level and not allowed to change suddenly. The adult fishes should be "conditioned" by feeding them live foods only.

Usually, you'll know that your live-bearers have produced young when you spot the tiny fry hiding among the aquatic plants in the tank. If you wish to raise as many of the young fish as possible, you should either remove the parent fish from the tank or place the babies in a smaller "nursery aquarium" for rearing. Keep the nursery tank warm—between 78 and 82 degrees—and feed the fry on very fine fish foods or baby brine shrimp.

Egg-layers are a bit tougher to breed in aquariums because they must have some kind of **spawning medium,** such as plants or rocks, among which to hide their eggs. Some of the more popular egg-laying tropical fishes are zebra danios, tiger barbs, convict cichlids, and Siamese fighting fish, or bettas. These species will easily breed in a home aquarium, though the eggs and young may be eaten by other fishes if the breeders are in a community tank.

Native egg-layers are generally too large as adults to be easily raised in home aquariums. And many species are more demanding than tropical

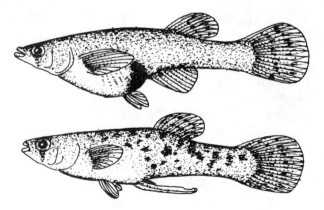

The gambusia, or mosquitofish. The top fish is female; the bottom is male.

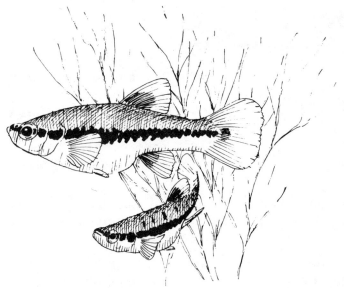

The least killifish.

fishes as far as tank conditions go. Some smaller native sunfishes, such as the black-banded, blue-spotted, and pygmy sunfishes, will build nests and lay eggs in an aquarium if they are not disturbed and the tank is large enough. Mudminnows and darters may spawn if they are kept by themselves in a roomy tank and fed lots of live brine shrimp and tubifex worms. Small catfishes such as madtoms may build nests if they have plenty of rocks and other hiding places in their tank. The brook and three-spined sticklebacks may build small, round nests of shredded plants if they are kept alone in a tank filled with aquatic plants.

All native fishes are much more likely to breed in an aquarium if they have lots of room and privacy and are given a varied and healthy diet.

The main rules to remember if you wish to try and breed egg-laying native fishes are:

✔ Experiment first with breeding easy tropical fishes, like guppies, platies, or zebra danios, so you get the hang of it before you try native fishes.

✔ Provide as large a breeding tank as you can. A 20-gallon aquarium or bigger is best for one or two pairs of breeders.

✔ Keep the breeding fish by themselves so they are not pestered by other fishes, or their eggs or young are not eaten.

✔ Study the natural habitat of the fish you'd like to breed, whether it's rocky, sandy, or weedy, and set up their tank in a similar way.

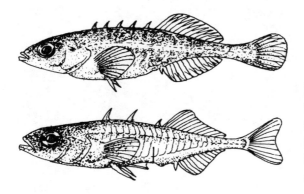

Both the brook (top) and the three-spined (bottom) sticklebacks will build nests of shredded plants in the aquarium if they are kept alone and not disturbed by other fishes.

✔ Do a partial change of about one-quarter of the tank's water (about 5 gallons in a 20-gallon tank) and condition your breeders with lots of live foods before spawning.

✔ Cover the aquarium with an observation cover and *do not disturb* the parents until the young fish are swimming about. You can observe the breeding activity through the observation slot. But try not to poke around in the tank while your fishes are spawning or taking care of very young fry. They may eat them if they are disturbed.

✔ Don't get discouraged if your fishes don't cooperate at first. Just keep them in the best condition possible and give them time! It's all part of the fun of native fishkeeping!

## 2. Aggression in Fishes

Nearly all fishes are territorial to one degree or another. Social fishes that school together in large groups still maintain a small "personal space" for themselves within the school. Solitary fishes that spend most of their time by themselves defend larger territories in their environment. A fish's territory, like your own home, provides shelter and protection in a dangerous world and can be vital to its survival.

Fish territories are usually set up around or near objects on the bottom, such as rocks, small caves, roots, or plants. A fish in its territory knows all of the objects that serve as its boundaries. It will chase away all other fishes that cross these borders. Even a small fish on its home territory feels very secure there and will chase off much larger fishes that invade its "turf." The larger fish knows that it is off its own territory and thus is insecure and can be chased away.

You can observe how aggressive behavior "comes and goes" in aquarium fishes using a simple method. Territorial fishes such as sunfishes or catfishes set up their territories by taking over a part of the tank. The fish may dig a small depression in the sand near a rock or use the space

Fish aggression. These two cichlids may look as though they are kissing, but they are actually struggling to settle the question of who's boss in the tank!

between rocks and plants, or even the aquarium filter as a home base. If you have several small sunfishes in your tank you'll see that, while they may squabble where their territory boundaries meet, each fish will seldom cross over into the other fish's territory.

If you change the appearance of one fish's territory even a little, however, a change in behavior will occur. Carefully reach into the tank and move a couple of the rocks or other decorations a few inches. At once, the fish holding that territory will become "homeless" because it no longer recognizes its personal space. It becomes confused and, as it wanders fearfully about and tries to hide in other fishes' territories, it will be chased by all of the other fishes in the aquarium. This situation is dangerous to the displaced fish only if the other fishes are large enough to injure it or eat it. Things will soon get back to normal in the aquarium as the homeless fish sets up a new territory and begins to guard it against trespassers.

Aquarium fishes become slightly mixed up every time an aquarist decides to rearrange the decorations in a tank. But most fishkeepers don't notice the little changes in behavior as things soon go back to normal. You might compare the fishes' annoyance to your own if someone goes into your room, which is *your* personal space, and changes it all around while you're away from it!

# Thinking Green:
## Aquatic Conservation and Recycling

Any hobby or activity that involves keeping wild creatures in captivity takes some toll on the natural world. Even the aquarium hobbyist who purchases all of his or her fishes at a pet shop and never "wets a net" in the actual capture of the fishes is directly responsible for removing animals from their natural environment. Many of the more popular tropical fish species are raised on fish farms in Florida and in Asia. But many species still cannot be cultured in captivity and are thus "wild caught." Professional fish collectors in South America, Southeast Asia, Africa, and the other tropical areas from which most of the popular aquarium fishes come would certainly not bother to go out and catch them if there was no market—and a large one—for pet fishes in the Western world. Collecting fishes for the pet trade is a multimillion dollar business today. Many questions have been asked about how much longer the natural environment can continue to supply the millions of fishes that are taken from it each year.

You might ask, then, "If removing wild fishes from their natural habitat and keeping them in aquariums is so bad for the environment, will my native fish collecting only make the situation worse?"

The answer to this important question is, no, if it's done right.

When we compare the many millions of tropical fishes collected each year for the aquarium trade with the few dozen native fishes a hobbyist may bring home in the same period of time—well, there's hardly any comparison at all. The effect of the loss of a few individual fishes on their ecosystem as a whole is practically nothing. Many more are lost to predators, disease, changing environmental conditions, and the many other perils any wild animal faces. The real threat to wild fishes is not anglers or aquarium fish collectors, but what biologists call *habitat degradation*.

Many individual fishes, and even entire populations of them, are disappearing in North America as their habitats are damaged or destroyed by pollution, acid rain, urban and agricultural development, and water-control projects. A healthy fish population in a healthy environment can easily withstand a good deal of fishing pressure and loss by predators. But if the environment itself is damaged or destroyed, the fishes will vanish along with it.

So just what *is* the answer to this problem?

Since we cannot deny that those few fishes a hobbyist captures for the aquarium are *still* removed from their lake, pond, or stream home, the whole situation boils down to two questions: "What is the overall effect of their removal from the habitat?" "Do the benefits of keeping them outweigh the cost to the environment?"

Here, the answer becomes a lot more upbeat. Collecting native fishes for aquarium use is worth the very small cost to the environment *if* those fishes make the fishkeeper appreciate the endangered aquatic world and want to help protect it. It's as simple as that.

Fishes and other aquatic creatures are in big trouble today partly because many people are unaware of them and their value to the environment. We're easily upset about the loss of elephants, eagles, whooping cranes, and timber wolves, and we're inspired to try to help save them from extinction. These are very conspicuous and attractive creatures and they appeal to many people. But the gradual disappearance of fishes from a lake, river, or the sea often goes unnoticed because they are not as dramatic as the larger creatures and are often overlooked by the majority of people. Most Americans and Canadians have very little idea of the variety of fish life found in the fresh waters of their countries and generally think that a supply of clean water is important only to human life. Many people, in fact, may be upset to learn that fishes actually live in the water they drink. They forget that if a fish couldn't live in it, it wouldn't be safe to drink!

If people aren't aware of the complex and wonderful world that stands to be lost if a lake or a river is dammed or polluted, it's hard for them to become involved in efforts to prevent the loss, or care one way or another. This has long been one of the major obstacles to aquatic preservation. More people need to be aware of the wonderful variety of life that lives below the water's surface. They need to know that if we destroy our freshwater habitats by pollution and changing them through dams and development, pure drinking water will not be the only loss, but the entire aquatic web of life.

The public relations problem is especially bad when it comes to freshwater habitats. Much more publicity has been given to ocean pollution and the threat to the often larger and more colorful creatures that live in it. Animals such as whales, sharks, and colorful coral reef fishes are frequently seen in television nature specials. They are much more familiar to the average person than the musk turtles, pickerels, mudminnows, and shiners that may be disappearing as their lake or river habitats are polluted or destroyed just a few miles away! It's easy to get angry over whalers killing humpback whales, but tougher to be concerned about the slow disappearance of creek chubs or madtom catfishes, which most people have never seen. But the humpback whale is no more a vital part of its ocean environment than the little madtom is of its stream home. Each living creature serves a purpose, however small or great it may be.

Part of the problem is that we just don't know what happens to all those complex links in the great web of life when any one kind of animal is suddenly removed from it forever. It may take many years before we fully realize what the loss of a single species of small animal, even a minnow, means to the health of its whole ecosystem.

This is where awareness comes in. It is one of the best reasons for the hands-on experience of native fishkeeping. Collecting your own fishes will give you an environmental education no trip to the pet shop ever can. And if you are a nature watcher at heart, a day in the field will offer observations of many plants and animals other than the fishes you are after. Fish collecting is actually a minisafari to a small wilderness near home!

You cannot avoid removing a fish from its natural habitat once you've made the decision to keep it at home in an aquarium and study it. But you *can* make the experience environmentally friendly and worth the small loss to the habitat in a number of ways. The two most obvious ways of keeping environmental loss to a minimum are (1) to collect only as many fishes as you really need to stock your tank and release the rest, and (2) whenever possible, to make native fishkeeping a recycling project.

Tropical fish hobbyists sometimes "recycle" fishes that have grown too large or are too aggressive. They bring them back to the pet shop in the hope that the store will take the fish in exchange for some fish foods, equipment, or another fish. Native freshwater fishes can be returned to their natural habitats with little trouble and no bad effects on the environment, as long as you don't live far from the place you caught them. Even native fishes should not simply be dumped into any handy lake or stream if it is far from the place they came from. The species may not be found naturally in the waters of your area. By releasing it there, you may cause trouble in your local aquatic ecosystem.

The question of *when* you return your native fishes to their natural habitat is also important. Obviously, fishes kept indoors in a room-temperature aquarium cannot be released in the middle of January unless you live in Florida or southern California! In more northern states that have cold winters, always plan ahead if you feel you will not be keeping your fishes for a year or more. Don't wait until the weather is too cold to release them. Fishes released into a natural habitat that is much cooler than the water of their aquarium cannot adapt to these conditions, no matter how long you might try to "reverse acclimate" them. They will have little chance of survival in the wild.

One of the best ways to make native fishkeeping more meaningful and rewarding is to record your observations of your captive fishes and assemble your notes into a personal journal, or a school report. You could even have your observations published. Aquarium magazines are often interested in well-written articles on native fishes in captivity. Surprisingly little is known about the habits and spawning of many North American fishes, especially those smaller species that are not important as game fishes. If you're handy with a camera, it can also be interesting to take "tank shots" of your native fishes. Any personal observation of native fishes has great value if shared with others, especially since some fish species are declining and there is still not much information on them.

Several aquarium publications are listed in Appendix 3 of this book. The native fishkeeper interested in a career in the aquatic sciences is encouraged to subscribe to one or more of them.

Other ways in which to "think green" when you're out collecting fishes are:

✔ Be careful of vegetation when walking along stream banks or lake shores. Shoreside plants help keep the soil from washing into a waterway. If it is trampled or destroyed, erosion may take place there.

✔ Take a plastic garbage bag along on a collecting trip and use it to bag any trash or litter you may find while you're there. You'll be surprised and disturbed to find litter even in the most secluded places. It will give you a real sense of satisfaction to leave a habitat in better shape than when you found it.

✔ Avoid collecting fishes in areas where they are observed spawning or guarding nests. Many sunfishes, in particular, are reluctant to leave their nests and can often be easily netted. This leaves the eggs or very young fry exposed to predators and is bad conservation practice!

✔ If you change the stream bed or lake bottom near shore by moving rocks to build fish traps, break up the trap and scatter the rocks about before you leave. Leaving a stream trap in place unnaturally restricts the movements of fishes and may make them more vulnerable to predators.

# Appendix 2

# The Golden Rules of Fishkeeping

Here are some aquarium-keeping words of wisdom that have been passed down through many generations of aquarists. If you follow these four, common-sense rules, as well as the Dos and Don'ts listed below them, you should experience little or no trouble and frustration in your native fishkeeping adventure!

## 1. Don't Overcrowd

This is Rule #1 of the aquarium hobby, because more problems stem from keeping too many fishes in too small an aquarium than from all other factors combined. Environmental crowding creates stress in fishes, just as it does among people. Fishes react in the same way as people do when they are crowded together: They become much more aggressive, tense, and irritable; they may lose their appetite and stay in hiding as much as possible; and they are more vulnerable to illness and disease. An aquarium in which there is constant aggressive activity, such as chasing and fighting, as well as sick or terrified fishes hiding among the plants or in the tank's corners, is almost certainly a badly overcrowded one!

Remember, limit your tank's fish population to the old "1 inch of fish per 1 gallon of water" and you can't go wrong!

## 2. Don't Overfeed

It isn't always easy to determine when you're overfeeding your fishes, because most healthy fishes will avidly eat food whenever it is offered to them. The obvious overfeeding gauge is if there is a good deal of food either floating on the water's surface or lying on the bottom after your fishes have eaten their fill, too much food is being offered. Overfeeding may be less obvious in a larger tank with many plants and decorations. The fishes may *appear* to eat everything given them several times a day. But much of the excess food may drift out of sight behind rocks, plants, and other objects, and the problem won't make itself known until the water turns gray and cloudy and begins to smell bad.

The rule of thumb here is feed the fishes twice a day and only what they can eat in 5 or 6 minutes. If you have a cloudy tank problem and you *know* that you're not exceeding this feeding schedule, someone else may be quietly feeding the fishes because "they seemed hungry." It's a common human urge to feed pets as often as they demand food, even if overfeeding may not be good for them. The trick is not to leave fish foods readily handy for "Good Samaritan" fish feeders. Other than that, about all you can do is inform other family members or friends about the dangers of overfeeding and request that they do not feed your fishes every time they pass by the tank!

# 3. Keep Compatible Tankmates

Surprisingly, many aquarists, especially beginning ones, are almost completely unaware that most fishes, even those pretty tropical fishes sold in stores, are meat-eating predators that will eat other fishes if they can. Many people who keep fishes will often unknowingly keep large predatory fishes with the same smaller fishes they would eat in the wild, unless an informed pet shop person warns them of the danger.

*Make sure* you are familiar with the habits and requirements of the native fishes you collect before you keep them together in an aquarium. Try to collect fishes that are all about the same size, for even basically peaceful fishes that are of a large size may bully much smaller fishes kept with them. Never keep more than one or two fishes that are *known* to be aggressive predators, such as bass or pickerel, in a smaller tank. These species are often intolerant of others of their own kind and will fight constantly. And, finally, try to provide plenty of hiding places for shyer species to escape any aggressive tankmates. These can be plant thickets, rock grottoes, old flower pots sunk in the sand, or waterlogged roots.

# 4. Make Regular Water Changes

The wise practice of making periodic water changes in an aquarium is often put off or forgotten entirely in this busy day and age. A water change using aged fresh water can "refresh" a tank and remove some of the impurities and wastes that the filtration system has not entirely eliminated.

In a healthy, balanced aquarium, water changes need only be made about once a month. Between 15 and 25 percent of the tank's water should be replaced with new water. This means that in the average 20-gallon aquarium, between 3 and 5 gallons of the water should be siphoned out and replaced with fresh water of the same chemistry and temperature. When making water changes, take advantage of the opportunity to siphon out all debris and wastes you see on the bottom and give the aquarium glass a good going-over with the algae scraper. Many aquarists report that immediately following a water change their fishes become more active and acquire brighter colors. The change obviously does them some good—sort of like getting a breath of fresh air!

# Dos and Don'ts

Here are a few pointers to help you avoid problems in your native fishes hobby and to give you the most enjoyment out of your aquatic adventure!

**DO** make sure your aquarium is large enough for the number of fishes you are interested in keeping.

**DO** study the habits and habitat requirements of the wild fishes you'll be collecting so you can give them the best living quarters possible in the home tank.

**DO** resist the temptation to bring home a lot of fishes; the fewer and healthier, the better.

**DO** take your time in acclimating your wild fishes to the aquarium. All wild creatures suddenly placed in a smaller environment need plenty of time to get over the stress of capture and the strangeness of aquarium life.

**DO** plan to make the native fish hobby a recycling experience. When possible, enjoy and observe your wild fishes for a period of time and then release them back into the natural habitat. It's a nice feeling to be able to successfully "keep and release."

**DON'T** be talked into purchasing aquarium equipment that is too expensive or too complicated to be easily maintained or operated, especially if you are a beginner. Start out with simple air pumps and corner filters and work your way up when you have gained experience and confidence with the hardware.

**DON'T** try to move an aquarium that has water in it, even a few inches. Water and wet sand can be very heavy. If the tank is handled incorrectly, it may split a seam and leak later on.

**DON'T** forget daily and weekly tank maintenance. A well set up aquarium is a thing of beauty in a home. But a neglected tank can become an eyesore and a nuisance to others. Keep a close eye on the operation of the filtration system, watch for sick or dead fishes, scrape any algae from the front glass weekly, and keep the aquarium securely covered to prevent fishes from ending up "on the carpet" or any aeration spray from damaging the walls or floor.

**DON'T** ignore conservation laws or good behavior standards when you're out collecting. Make sure the fishes you're after can be collected legally, always ask permission when collecting on private property, avoid leaving litter or overturned rocks behind, and always talk about conservation and care for the environment if curious bystanders approach and ask, "Whatcha doing?"

# Appendix 3

# Places to Observe and Study Fishes
## (and Other Aquatic Animals)

## Public Aquariums

**Aquarium of the Americas**
One Canal St.
New Orleans, LA
(504)861–2538

**The Aquarium for Wildlife**
 **Conservation**
W. 8th St. & Surf Ave.
 Brooklyn, NY 11224
(718)265–3400

**Belle Isle Zoo & Aquarium**
Detroit Zoo
Box 39
Royal Oak, MI 48068
(313)267–7160

**Dallas Aquarium**
Box 26193
Dallas, TX 75226
(214)670–8441

**Marine World Africa USA**
Marine World Parkway
Vallejo, CA 94589
(707)644–4000

**Monterey Bay Aquarium**
886 Cannery Row
Monterey, CA 93904
(408)649–6466

**Mystic Marinelife Aquarium**
Coogan Blvd.
Mystic, CT 06355
(203)536–9631

**National Aquarium in Baltimore**
Pier 3, 501 East Pratt St.
Baltimore, MD 21202
(301)576–3800

**New England Aquarium**
Central Wharf
Boston, MA 02110
(617)973–5200

**Thomas H. Kean (New Jersey**
 **State) Aquarium**
Camden, NJ 08102
(609)365–3300

**Sea Life Park**
Makapuu Point
Waimanalo, HI 96795
(808)259–7933

**Sea World of California**
1720 S. Shores Rd.
San Diego, CA 92109
(619)222–6362

**Sea World of Florida**
7007 Sea World Dr.
Orlando, FL 32821
(305)351–3600

**Sea World of Ohio**
1100 Sea World Dr.
Aurora, OH 44202
(216)562–8101

**The Seattle Aquarium**
Pier 59, Waterfront Park
Seattle, WA 98101
(206)625–4358

**John G. Shedd Aquarium**
1200 S. Lake Shore Dr.
Chicago, IL 60605
(312)939–2426

**Steinhart Aquarium**
Golden Gate Park
San Francisco, CA
(415)221–5100

**Stephen Birch Aquarium Museum**
2300 Expedition Way
La Jolla, CA 92093
(619)534–FISH

**Vancouver Public Aquarium**
Box 3232, Vancouver, B.C.
Canada V6B 3X8
(604)685–3364

**Waikiki Aquarium**
2777 Kalakaua Ave.
Honolulu, HI 96815
(808)923–5335

## Native Fishes Organizations

**The American Littoral Society**
Sandy Hook
Highlands, NJ 07732

**Coastal Conservation Association**
4801 Wood Way & 220 West
Houston, TX 77056

**Desert Fishes Council**
407 West Line St.
Bishop, CA 93514

**International Marinelife
   Alliance–Canada**
2883 Otterson Dr.
Ottawa, Ontario K1V 7B2
Canada

**International Marinelife
   Alliance–USA**
94 Station St., Suite 645
Hingham, MA 02043

**Native American Fish and Wildlife
   Society**
750 Burbank St.
Broomfield, CO 80020

**North American Native Fishes
   Association**
123 West Mount Airy Ave.
Philadelphia, PA 19119

## Aquarium Magazines

**American Currents**
The North American Native Fishes
  Association
123 West Mount Airy Ave.
Philadelphia, PA 19119

**Tropical Fish Hobbyist**
One TFH Plaza
Neptune, NJ 07753

**Freshwater and Marine Aquarium
  Magazine**
120 West Sierra Madre Blvd.
Sierra Madre, CA 91024

**Aquarium Fish Magazine**
P. O. Box 484
Mount Morris, IL 61054

**Underwater Naturalist**
The American Littoral Society
Sandy Hook
Highlands, NJ 07732

# Glossary

**Acclimatization.** The process by which a fish is gradually introduced into an aquarium.

**Aeration.** The forced introduction of oxygen into the water by bubble action.

**Aerobic.** Oxygen-requiring.

**Air-line tubing.** Plastic tubing through which air is delivered to the aquarium filters and air stones.

**Airstone.** A porous block fitted to the end of the air line to produce a mist of bubbles.

**All-glass tank.** A frameless aquarium made of five sheets of glass secured together with silicone cement.

**Ambush predator.** An animal that hides and waits for prey to come to it.

**Anal fin.** Fin located on the fish's underside just forward of the tail.

**Aquarist.** A person who keeps fishes for pleasure or scientific study.

**Backwater.** Quiet pool at the side of a stream or river.

**Bar.** A ridge of sand or gravel in a stream or the sea formed by currents.

**Barbel.** Short fleshy projection near a fish's mouth. Used to find food.

**Biological filtration.** A filtration system that uses the action of bacteria in the filtering medium to remove impurities from the aquarium.

**Bottom fishes.** Fishes that live on or near the bottom, or substrate.

**Buoyancy.** The degree to which an object floats or sinks in water.

**Brine shrimp.** A tiny crustacean living in salt or brackish water that is a very popular live food for aquarium fishes.

**Carnivorous.** A meat eater; feeds on other animals.

**Caudal fin.** The tail, the fin at the rear of a fish's body.

**Caudal peduncle.** The rear, slender part of the fish's body at the base of the caudal fin, or tail.

**Coastal Plain.** The flat plain extending inland from the sea along the Atlantic and Gulf coasts.

**Coldwater fishes.** Fishes from more temperate regions that do not require a heater in their tank.

**Community tank.** An aquarium in which fishes of many different species are kept together.

**Countershading.** When an object or animal is colored darker above and lighter below; the opposite of normal shading.

**Crustacean.** Segmented animals with jointed limbs and hard outer shells.

**Deep-bodied fishes.** Fishes in which the body is wide and flattened from side to side.

**Detritus.** Natural organic matter that gathers on the bottom of an aquarium.

**Dissipation.** Gradually decreasing through evaporation.

**Dorsal.** The upper side of the fish.

**Dorsal fin.** The fin, or fins, located on the back of a fish.

**Ear flap.** A fleshy tab on the gill cover of a fish, especially sunfishes.

**Eel-like fishes.** Fishes that have long, snakelike or eel-like bodies.

**Field of view.** The area an animal can see without moving its head or eyes.

**Filter medium.** The material through which aquarium water is pumped and dirt is removed. It can be charcoal, glass wool, or sponge material.

**Filtration.** The process of removing waste material from aquarium water.

**Fish/Fishes.** Cold-blooded vertebrate animals with fins and gills that live in water. In the plural: *fish* means many fish of the same species; *fishes* means many fishes of different species.

**Freshet.** A stream or rush of fresh water that flows into the ocean.

**Freshwater fishes.** Fish that are native to water that contains no salt.

**Fry.** The young of fishes.

**Gill.** The breathing organ in fishes.

**Gill cover.** Bony flap covering the gills in a fish's head.

**Habitat.** The place where fishes or other animals live.

**Hand net.** A small net usually used to move fishes from one container to another.

**Hardness.** The amount of dissolved minerals in water.

**Herbivorous.** A vegetarian; feeds on plants.

**Hydrologic cycle.** The natural cycle in which water circulates from the atmosphere to the land, to the sea, and back to the atmosphere.

**Ichthyologist.** A person who studies fishes.

**Impeller.** The small wheel with blades that spins and moves water through a filter.

**Invertebrate.** Animals lacking a spine, or backbone.

**Juvenile.** The young of a fish species, usually a small version of the adult.

**Larva.** In fishes, a newborn fish; the stage before it becomes a juvenile.

**Lateral line.** A canal of pores along the fish's body that contains sense organs.

**Littoral zone.** Near or at the shoreline of a lake or the sea.

**Live-bearing fishes.** Fishes that give birth to living young rather than laying eggs.

**Live food.** Any smaller animals, usually invertebrates such as brine shrimp, that are fed alive to fishes.

**Marine.** Pertaining to the saltwater environment.

**Nocturnal.** Active mostly at night.

**Omnivorous.** Eating meats or vegetables and plants.

**Operculum.** The bony cover of the gill chamber that contains a fish's breathing organs.

**Pectoral fins.** A pair of fins attached to the shoulder of a fish, just behind the head.

**Pelagic.** Living in open water.

**Pelvic fins.** A pair of usually small fins on the lower part of a fish's body; also called the *ventral fins*.

**Pool.** A quiet, often deep part of a stream or river.

**Power filter.** A mechanical filter with a high flow rate, usually driven by an electric motor with an impeller.

**Protective coloration.** An animal's colors and patterns that help make it less visible in its environment.

**Reflector.** Aquarium cover that contains light fixtures.

**Riffle.** Fast-flowing, shallow part of a stream.

**Rover-predator.** A fish that swims actively about in search of prey.

**Run.** Part of a stream between a riffle and a deeper pool; it is usually a little slower and deeper than a riffle.

**Scavenger.** An animal that seeks out and eats food left by other animals.

**Schooling.** Behavior in which fish of the same species gather in large groups and swim together.

**Seine.** A rectangular net up to about 100 feet that is dragged through the water to catch fishes and other aquatic animals.

**Single-species tank.** An aquarium in which one species of fish, usually a very aggressive or very shy species, is kept.

**Siphon tube.** Plastic tube or device used to transfer water from one container to another.

**Snout.** Part of a fish's head in front of the eyes and above the mouth.

**Spawning.** The term used for fish-breeding activity.

**Spawning medium.** Any surface, such as rocks or plants, on which fishes lay their eggs.

**Species.** A group of similar animals capable of interbreeding and producing fertile offspring.

**Subspecies.** A population of animals that is different from the main species or lives separated from it.

**Substrate.** The bottom of a lake, stream, or ocean, or the material used to cover the bottom of an aquarium.

**Subterminal mouth.** When the fish's mouth opens below the point of the head.

**Surface area.** The amount of the water's surface in contact with the atmosphere.

**Surface swimmer.** A fish that lives at or near the surface of the water.

**Swim bladder.** A gas-filled organ that allows the fish to adjust its ability to float or sink in the water.

**Territoriality.** When an animal defends a certain area against others.

**Tropical fishes.** Fishes from warm regions that require a heated aquarium.

**Tubercle.** A small, hard point or bump on a fish's skin, usually appearing on or near the head at spawning time.

**Upturned mouth.** When a fish's mouth opens above the point of the snout.

**Ventral fins.** The paired fins on the underside of the fish; also called the *pelvic fins.*

**Vertebrate.** An animal having a spine, or backbone.

**Water surface.** In fishkeeping, the area of the tank's water that is exposed to air so that harmful gases can escape from it and oxygen can enter it. Also called *surface area.*

# Index